UNDERSTANDING
JEWISH HISTORY

from the Renaissance to the 21st Century

Sol Scharfstein

design & graphics by
Dorcas Gelabert

KTAV Publishing House, Inc.
Hoboken, N. J.

This book
is lovingly dedicated
to my parents
Asher and Feiga
of
blessed memory

Copyright © 1997
KTAV Publishing House, Inc.

Understanding Jewish History, Part II: From the Renaissance to the 21st Century
ISBN 0-88125-560-2

The Library of Congress has cataloged volume 1 as follows:

Scharfstein, Sol. 1921–
    Understanding Jewish History / Sol Scharfstein ; design & graphics by Dorcas Gelabert.
        p.   cm.
    Includes index.
    Contents: 1. From the Patriarchs to the expulsion from Spain.
    ISBN 0-88125-545-9 (paper)
    1. Jews—History—Juvenile literature. I. Gelabert, Dorcas. II. Title.
DS118.S3176   1996
909'.04924—dc20   96-11250
                                                                           CIP

Manufactured in Hong Kong

Contents

Contents

Contents

Introduction and Acknowledgments

Introduction

It all began about 4,000 years ago in the ancient city of Ur, in what is now Iraq. Divinely inspired, Abraham and his wife Sarah, the first patriarch and matriarch, began a saga that produced the best of times and the worst of times for their descendants–the Jews.

Understanding Jewish History records the many stories of the journey of the Jewish people through the annals of history. It is a story filled with triumphs and defeats, joys and tragedies, destruction and rebuilding, and lastly, Holocaust and rebirth. The countless struggles conferred a historic immortality on some individuals and places scattered through a myriad of kingdoms and countries.

From the beginning, the Jewish homeland, Israel, was at the crossroads of many civilizations and was dominated by powerful nations. Yet, despite the overpowering foreign influences, the Jewish people managed to survive as a national entity. Even in exile, they miraculously retained their cohesiveness and their peoplehood.

There never was any doubt about what they were fighting for or whether their obstinancy was worth the price. They fought to retain the right to worship as they pleased and to maintain their own unique way of life.

Unfortunately, for thousands of years Jews were not masters of their own history. Defeats, dispersions, and expulsions scattered them throughout the world. More than any other people they have been actors in historical theaters other than their own. As Jews and as foreigners they were dependent on the events, politics, poverty, prosperity, and personalities of the dominant power.

Mostly, and especially during the Middle Ages, Jews were the pawns on the chessboard of power politics. When their usefulness ended, they became as scapegoats to divert the masses from their misery and powerlessness.

The Text

Understanding Jewish History 2 is a short, readable history of the Jewish people. It contains 149 one- and two-page historical essays, illustrated with colorful photographs, action maps, and explanatory charts. Each of the photographs is accompanied by a comprehensive caption which provides additional information.

Introduction and Acknowledgments

Timelines
Understanding Jewish History also contains six colorful, illustrated Timelines. They present a compact record of Jewish history extending from the Renaissance to the final years of the 20th century. Each two-page unit, is a stand-alone, three-dimensional panoramic display featuring dates, places, events, personalities, and Jewish scholarly texts. Its format enables the reader to grasp the continuity and flow of Jewish history as well as its position in the general history of the host country or geographical area.

Understanding Jewish History: Part 2
Part 2 starts with the Renaissance and continues up to the Oslo Agreements between Israel and the Palestine Liberation Organization.

Acknowledgments
Numerous talented people have worked hard to bring *Understanding Jewish History* to life. They believed in the project and labored long and arduously, critiquing, editing, updating, and researching.

I wish to thank the following for their expert assistance. It is their sense, sensibility, sensitivity, and scholarship that have shaped the text.

Howard Adelman
Yaakov Elman
Robert Milch
Richard White

The final responsibility for any omissions, errors, and mistakes is my own.

The Renaissance

The Coming of a New Age

The 15th and 16th centuries—the period during which the tragic expulsion of the Jews from Spain and Portugal took place—witnessed many great social, technical, and religious changes.

New inventions radically transformed life everywhere. One of these was the printing press. As a result of the increased availability of books, people became more interested in learning and many were eager to read the Bible. Indeed, the Bible (in Latin) was the first book to be printed. This revolutionary first edition was produced in 1456 by a German printer, Johann Gutenberg, in the city of Mayence (Mainz). Many scholars now wanted to read the Bible in the original language, and they turned to Jewish teachers in their efforts to learn Hebrew.

Jews, too, enthusiastically took up the craft of printing. Jewish immigrants from Germany brought it to Italy, where the first printed Hebrew book, an edition of Tractate Berakhot of the Talmud, was published in 1484 by Joshua Solomon Soncino. Many other Hebrew works soon followed.

New Ideas

The Jews of Italy were greatly stimulated by the free spirit of the Renaissance. Just as Christian writers, poets, composers, artists, and scientists began to express new ideas and a new view of the world, many Jewish artists and scientists also became active. Despite the restrictive laws still in force against Jews during the early Renaissance, the Jewish communities of Italy flourished.

In the Netherlands, struggling to win independence from Spain, and in Germany, France, and eventually England, the spirit of the Renaissance stimulated the growth of

Emblem of the Venetian printer Marco Antonio Giustinani.

An illuminated page from Gutenberg's Bible.

new life. All over Europe the misty Middle Ages were coming to an end.

The Reformation

In Germany the new learning gave rise to a religious movement known as the Reformation. Martin Luther, the first to translate the Bible into German, opposed the power of the Catholic Church and strove to replace it with a reformed form of Christianity. Luther, Calvin, Zwingli, and other reformers were the founders of Protestant denominations which taught that every individual human being had a personal relationship with God and could find his way to God without the help of intermediaries.

Martin Luther, as depicted by the artist Lucas Cranach.

The Shtadlanim

The rulers of Europe in the 17th and 18th centuries needed people who were loyal and had the skills to supply their financial needs.

They also needed people to represent them on confidential diplomatic missions, provide military supplies, and supply difficult-to-locate luxury items. This delicate and difficult role was often filled by court Jews (*shtadlanim*), who were dependent upon the monarch for protection and remained neutral in the power struggles raging between the clergy, nobles, and rising expectations of the general populace. The presence of a shtadlan at a royal court helped the Jews return to cities and countries from which they had been expelled.

Shtadlanim were the spokesmen for the Jewish community in dealings with town councils and governments. The shtadlanim sought to prevent persecution and defended the interests of the Jewish community. Some were rabbis, others were linguists, and some had widespread business connections and diplomatic skills.

Some of the shtadlanim used their skills and connections to establish banks and trading companies. A great many had far-flung financial connections with Jewish and non-Jewish commercial and industrial trading houses.

Joseph Suess Oppenheimer

Court Jews faced great opportunities and great dangers. Samuel Oppenheimer (1630–1703) loyally served Emperor Leopold I of Austria for 30 years, yet died penniless.

Joseph Suess Oppenheimer (1698–1738)

Joseph Suess Oppenheimer (1698–1738) was shtadlan for Duke Charles I Alexander of Wuerttemberg, managing his estates and business enterprises.

After the duke's death, Jude Suess, as he was called, was imprisoned and hanged in a public ceremony. Oppenheimer refused the offers of the clergy to save his life on the condition that he convert to Christianity. He died reciting the Shema Yisrael.

Yossel of Rosheim

The outstanding shtadlan of 16th-century German Jewry was Yosel (Josel or Joselmann) of Rosheim, a town in Alsace (1480–1554). When still a young boy, he had seen all the members of his family perish as martyrs. Yosel traveled throughout Germany to carry out the task entrusted to him—the defense of the Jewish communities against attack.

Yosel was an active and talented financier, with an excellent background of Jewish learning. In addition to his practical work on behalf of his people, he managed to write two scholarly works, and in the course of his many diplomatic missions he engaged in debate with princes and priests who attacked the Talmud and other Jewish writings.

During the reign of Charles V, ruler of the Holy Roman Empire, when the Jewish communities were threatened with persecution and expulsion by both the Catholics and the Protestants, Yosel traveled hundreds of miles on diplomatic missions. He was not always successful, but many communities owed their peace and indeed their very lives to his efforts. The great community of Prague, in Bohemia, was saved from expulsion by Yosel. He kept a diary in which he recorded many of his experiences during his 40 years as shtadlan of the Jews of Germany. These notes have been preserved to this day.

The lives of Yosel of Rosheim, the Jewish shtadlan, and Martin Luther, the leader of the German Protestant Reformation, covered almost the same span: Luther's from 1483 to 1546 and Yosel's from 1480 to 1554.

Jost Liebmann was a shtadlan in the court of King Frederick William I of Prussia. When he died his wife Esther inherited the position and became the shatadlanit. However, after the death of her benefactor, King Frederick William, she was imprisoned and fined for accumulating excessive profits.

These were stormy times, during which the lands of Western Europe were faced with a challenging crisis—the struggle between the Roman Catholic Church and the Reformation.

Anti-Semitic picture of Yosel of Rosheim, the Court Jew of Emperor Charles V. In one hand is a Hebrew Bible, in the other, a bag of money.

Yet, behind their ghetto walls, following their own traditions and their own way of life, Jews weathered the storms of the centuries that followed, the struggles between Christians, between the church and princes, and the wars and revolutions set off by the new conditions and new ideas.

The public hanging of Joseph Suess Oppenheimer, whose corpse was then displayed in an iron cage. The anti-Semites used accusations against Oppenheimer to spread their message of hate.

The Ghetto

During the Renaissance Jews were forced to live in segregated districts. Residential areas of this kind were called ghettos, probably because the first of them, established in Venice, was located next to a cannon factory and was designated with the Italian word for "factory," *getto*. Some, however, believe that ghetto comes from the Hebrew word *get*, meaning "divorce," indicating that ghettoization separated and divorced the Jews from the general population.

Pope Paul IV

Paul IV argued that it was foolish for Christians to be friendly to a people who had not accepted Christ as their savior. In a papal bull he decreed that Jews living in areas controlled by the church were to be confined in ghettos. They would be permitted to leave the ghetto in daytime to go to work, but forbidden to be outside at other times. The ghetto gates were to be closed at night and on Christian holidays. The pope also decreed that Jews were to wear yellow stars and pointed hats for quick identification. In a short time these practices spread from Italy to the rest of Europe.

The ghetto was usually located in the worst part of town. The ghetto walls confined a large number of Jews into a small confined area. To accommodate this mass of humanity, houses were multistoried and built close to each other. The ghettos were surrounded by a wall and gates, guarded by non-Jewish watchmen who controlled the entry and exit of those imprisoned inside. Outside the ghetto Jews had to wear yellow badges and specially designed hats. These opened them to ridicule and attack.

Economic Restrictions

Economic regulations reduced the ability of Jews to earn a livelihood. Restrictions on commerce and banking deprived them of the ability to compete. Only two occupations were unrestricted: trade in second-hand merchandise and pawnbroking. People who for one reason or another needed a small loan brought something to sell or to leave in pawn. Poor people were thankful for a chance to buy good second-hand clothing cheaply. However, the Christian merchants who sold expensive new clothing objected to the competition.

The Forces for Ghetto Existence

There are several reasons why the ghetto came into existence and for its popularity in Europe. The expulsion from Spain triggered the idea that Jews should not be permitted to live in a Christian country.

In 1417 the Jews of Constance, Germany, offered a Torah scroll to Pope Martin V, with a request that their privilege be restored. He replied, "You have the law but do not understand it. The old has passed away and the new has been found."

While Christian merchants and artisans wanted to eliminate their Jewish competitors, government officials saw the Jews as a source of income and did not wish to expel them. The installation of the ghetto was an ideal compromise.

A third reason was related to the religious competition between Catholics and Protestants. Both groups competed by teaching hatred of the Jews. The Catholics, in fact, often accused the Protestants of favoring the Jews and being under their influence.

Starting in the 15th century, these three forces had an important detrimental effect on Jewish life in Eastern and Western Europe.

The Communal Structure

Ghetto communities were usually governed by a council elected by the residents. The council was responsible for the ghetto's relations with the city government, and in particular was charged with collecting whatever taxes the government levied on the Jews. In addition it supervised the ghetto's synagogue, schools, courts, charities, and other communal institutions.

Medieval painting of a Hebrew teacher and his young pupil. Notice the whip and the hourglass. Germany, 13th cent.

Gate of the Jewish ghetto in Vienna.

Painting by Hieronymus Hess, in the art museum of Basel, Switzerland. The Jews were forced to attend conversion sermons by Catholic priests. Note the priest slapping a Jew for snickering or for falling asleep.

Religious Intolerance

Protestants and Catholics

The new Protestant denominations that came to life in the Reformation had separated themselves from the Roman Catholic Church and now represented a grave threat to its unity. As a result, the church adopted stern measures to guard against the spread of Reformation influences.

Protestants and Catholics became involved in a bitter struggle, each faction bent on proving itself more truly Christian than the other and vying with the other in performing pious acts. Both Catholic and Protestant rulers persecuted heretics and imposed new restrictions on the Jews.

Wherever Jews were permitted to live in Western and Central Europe, except in the tolerant Netherlands, there were ghettos. Jews were set apart and crowded into these confined residential areas, their freedom restricted. Of course, the bait of conversion was always held out to anyone who would accept it. But nearly all Jews disregarded this alternative and steadfastly clung to the heritage of their ancestors.

The Jews of Italy

Although ghetto walls had been erected in Italy, the Italian Jews lived under far better conditions than did their brethren in the rest of Europe. Sometimes, they became traders or bankers, although their commercial activities were restricted, as was true all over Europe, to moneylending and the second-hand trade. According to some scholars, the family of Christopher Columbus was among them.

Italy attracted persecuted Jews from both Spain and Germany. Spanish Jewish merchants, seafarers, mapmakers, doctors, bankers, and scholars all settled in Italy. Jewish printers from Germany settled in northern Italy, where they produced editions of the Talmud, the Bible, and the prayerbook. The most famous of these printers was the Soncino family, whose name was revived by a group of Jewish bibliophiles in Germany before World War II, and adopted by a London publishing house that still prints Jewish books, including an English translation of the entire Talmud.

Jews fared best in the Kingdom of Naples, where Don Isaac Abravanel and many other Spanish Jews found a new home after the expulsion in 1492.

A street in the Jewish ghetto in Venice.

Hebrew emblem of the Italian printer Abraham Usque.

Title page of Don Isaac Abravanel's commentary to the Later Prophets.

The Jews of Turkey

In the 14th and 15th centuries the Ottoman Turks conquered Anatolia, the Fertile Crescent, and many European lands, including Greece, Albania, Bulgaria, Rumania, Bosnia, and Serbia. Their capture of Constantinople in 1453 ended the long history of the Byzantine Empire.

There had been Jews living in the Ottoman territories since ancient times. After the expulsions from Spain and Portugal, their numbers were greatly increased by exiles seeking a new home, and in the 16th century a flourishing Jewish community developed in the Ottoman domain. The port of Salonica in northern Greece became a major center of Jewish life and commerce.

The Turkish sultans welcomed the Jewish merchants, bankers, and physicians from Spain, and put their talents to good use. Jews rose to high positions at the Ottoman court, serving as ambassadors and advisors.

Solomon Ashkenazi / 1520–1600

It was as if the golden age of Spanish rule had returned once more in the lands of the East. Jewish diplomats were sent from Constantinople to the courts of Europe. Solomon Ashkenazi, a learned Jewish physician, became Turkey's ambassador to Venice, where he negotiated a peace treaty in 1571. Later, he offered Turkey's help to Venice in case of war with Spain.

When the Jews of Venice were threatened with expulsion, Ashkenazi pressured the Venetian government to revoke the order. Thanks to his efforts, the Jewish community was saved.

The Mendes Family

Gracia Mendes (1510–1569) was a Portuguese Marrano who sought refuge in Italy. The beautiful widow of a wealthy and famous banker, she had taken over her husband's business after his death. When she left Portugal, she was accompanied by her daughter Reyna and her nephew and business advisor, Joseph Nasi. They had settled in the great port of Antwerp in Belgium, which was then under Spanish rule. But when they were denounced to the Inquisition as heretics, Gracia Mendes and her family fled from Antwerp and found refuge in Venice. There again Gracia Mendes was denounced as a heretic who had abandoned the Catholic Church. She was imprisoned and all her wealth was confiscated. Many of her debtors cancelled their obligations, including the king of France, who owed the Mendes family great sums of money, but declared he would not pay his debt.

Joseph Nasi was determined to rescue his aunt and his cousin. He went to Constantinople and enlisted the help of Sultan Suleiman I. The sultan, impressed by Joseph Nasi's ability and connections, sent a letter to Venice demanding the release of Gracia Mendes.

Doña Gracia Mendes

Joseph Nasi / 1520–1579

Thanks to the sultan's intervention, Gracia Mendes was released from prison and her confiscated property was returned. She went from Venice to Ferrara, where she openly rejoined the Jewish community. When her confiscated property was returned, she proved to be a generous and compassionate woman, giving much of her time and fortune to aid troubled Jews and Marranos who were returning to Judaism. From Ferrara, Gracia Mendes and her daughter journeyed on to Turkey, where Joseph Nasi and Reyna were married.

Joseph in Palestine

Joseph Nasi became the sultan's financial advisor. The young man's intelligence, tactful counsel, and charming manner made him one of the most respected personalities at the sultan's court. He became a skilled diplomat. His knowledge of languages and his connections in many lands made him an ideal diplomat, so that Joseph Nasi was appointed to represent Turkey in conferences with many foreign ambassadors.

After the death of Suleiman, Joseph served his son, Selim II. The new sultan heaped many honors upon Joseph. In addition to making him duke of Naxos, a beautiful island in the Aegean Sea, he granted him the ancient city of Tiberias, in Palestine, where once the rabbis of the Mishnah had taught. Joseph hoped that large numbers of Jews and Marranos would settle in Tiberias, where they would be free from fear and oppression, and could build a new life in the land of their ancestors.

Joseph Nasi's vision had a practical side. In Tiberias he hoped to found a new industry that would

bring profit to both the Jewish settlers and the Ottoman Empire—the manufacture of silk. He rebuilt the houses and streets of Tiberias, and planted mulberry trees for the silkworms to feed upon. However, his plans were not realized. Only a few Jews were able to reach the Holy Land, for a war had broken out between Venice and Turkey and ships could not sail the Mediterranean safely. Yet Joseph Nasi was not discouraged. At a time when few wealthy men put the ideals of charity into action, he continued to devote much of his wealth and energy to the service of his suffering brethren.

Suleiman the Magnificent receiving Christian vassals as his army besieges the Hungarian town of Szigetvar.

View of Istanbul, 17th cent.

Pioneers and Mystics

Immigrants to Palestine

The dream of returning to the Land of Israel was ever present in the hearts of all Jews. On the ninth of Av, Jews everywhere wept and fasted in mourning for the destruction of the Temple. Throughout the centuries a trickle of Jewish settlers made their way to Palestine from Germany, France, Italy, and Turkey. In the aftermath of the expulsion from Spain, new immigration came to the ancient communities of Galilee in northern Palestine. A few of the Spanish refugees established themselves in Tiberias. Others went to Jerusalem, most beloved of the cities of the Holy Land. But it was in the town of Safed, in the mountains of Galilee, that the most renowned new community was founded.

Safed: City of the Kabbalah

In this poor little town, a new type of learning blossomed. Schools of mysticism arose, and rabbis steeped in arcane lore passed through the ancient streets discussing the deeper meaning of the Torah. Safed's scholars devoted themselves to the study of Kabbalah—the doctrines and lore of Jewish mysticism. The kabbalists of Safed were concerned primarily with questions relating to the coming of the Messiah. How could evil play such a predominant role in a world created by a benevolent God? What was the nature and means by which a transcendent God interacted with His limited creations?

Most important among the esoteric books that the kabbalists studied was the Zohar. To the kabbalists of Safed, Simeon bar Yohai, the tanna to whom the book was attributed, was a beloved figure. On Lag Ba-Omer, said to be the day of Simeon's death, the Jews of Safed made a pilgrimage to his grave in Meron to honor his memory with prayer, song, and dance. This practice is still followed in modern Israel.

The kabbalists of Safed sought the joy of intense contemplation and a pure life. On the Sabbath, they would dress in special garments and devote themselves to joyously celebrating the day of rest. The famous hymn Lekha Dodi, "Come, My Beloved," which is still chanted in the synagogue on Friday nights, was composed by Solomon Alkabetz (1505–1584), one of the great kabbalist teachers of Safed. In this poem he compared the Sabbath to a beautiful bride, and the people of Israel to her devoted bridegroom.

Lag Ba-Omer is celebrated on the 33rd day of the counting of the Omer. It is a time for singing, dancing, bonfires, picnics, hiking, and playing with bows and arrows.

On Lag Ba-Omer Jews remember the heroes who fought the Romans, especially Simeon bar Yohai. He and his son studied Torah in a cave high on Mount Meron. Students carried bows and pretended to be hunting so the Romans would not arrest them.

For 13 years Rabbi Simeon bar Yohai was hidden in his cave. This brave rabbi died on Lag Ba-Omer.

Today in Israel many Jews travel to Meron on foot and by car to visit his grave.

The Zohar

Moses de Leon / 1250–1305

The body of mystical lore that comprises the Kabbalah developed over several centuries. In the 13th century, all these teachings were compiled in a book called the Zohar by Moses de Leon of Castile, Spain. According to Moses de Leon, however, the Zohar dated back to the 2nd century C.E. and had been written by Simeon bar Yohai. He claimed to have found it in the cave in which Simeon bar Yohai and his son Eliezer had hidden for 13 years during the Hadrianic persecution. Throughout this period, the Talmud records, Simeon and his son ate the fruit of a carob tree and spent their time studying the mysteries of the Torah.

The Zohar fascinated Jewish scholars, and in the next few centuries interest in the Kabbalah spread from Spain to the other countries of the diaspora.

The Sefirot

The kabbalists maintained that every aspect of the Torah, even including the shapes of the letters and unusual spellings, has a secret meaning that can be uncovered through study and spiritual discipline. The hidden meanings embodied in the sacred text are set forth in the Zohar, written in Aramaic and organized as a commentary on the Torah.

The doctrine of the Sefirot has an important place in the Zohar. According to the mystics, there are ten divine aspects of God's interaction with the world; these mediate between between the Infinite God and the finite material universe. The ten Sefirot are:

Keter = Crown, Hokmah = Wisdom,
Binah = Understanding, Hesed=Mercy,
Gevurah = Strength, Tifarah = Beauty,Netzah = Might,
Hod = Splendor, Yesod = Foundation, Malkut = Kingdom.

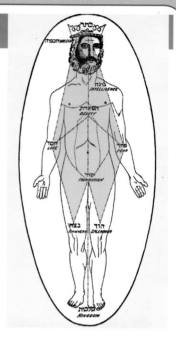

According to the Kabbalah, each of the Sefirot of the Tree of Life corresponds to a part of the human body. These power centers are energy spheres which control the physical, mental, and psychological functions of the human being. When they are operating properly they provide the individual with special abilities of perception and creativity.

The Zohar retells biblical stories and events, such as the creation of the world, the divine chariot of Ezekiel, the various names of God, and the powers of angels, explaining them in a mystical way.

In kabbalistic studies the Sefirot are combined, and the letters are then reassembled and given new meanings and significance.

Individual Responsibility

The Zohar also teaches that every act of every human being on earth has an effect on the world above. When we perform good deeds, we crown the day with goodness and it becomes our protection in the world-to-come and in our hour of need. But if we sin, it has a negative effect on the day and will destroy us in the world-to-come. Thus, good and bad deeds can build or destroy the balance of the earth.

Some of the formulas and symbols developed by the mystics have been utilized in the prayerbook. The blowing of the shofar is introduced with a kabbalistic prayer. The prayer before reading the Torah, the Berikh Shemei, is from the Zohar.

Rabbi Isaac Luria / 1534–1572

Rabbi Isaac Luria

The greatest teacher of Kabbalah in Safed was the brilliant young Rabbi Isaac Luria (1534–1572). Born in Jerusalem, he lost his father when he was a child but was brought to Cairo, where he was educated under the care of his uncle. Luria made rapid progress in his rabbinic studies and became acquainted with the Kabbalah, to which he applied himself fervently.

Magic formulas from *Sefer Raziel.* This kabbalistic book was printed in Amsterdam in 1701.

Kabbalistic alphabetic formulas in *Ilan Sefirot* ("A Tree of Emanation") by Abraham Cohen Herera, published about 1600.

When Rabbi Isaac Luria came to Safed, he found many devoted, enthusiastic students there. By devoting themselves to the joys of mystical speculation, prayer, and concentration, they hoped to hasten the coming of the Messiah and the time of eternal peace. Rabbi Luria's charismatic personality and unique approach to kabbalistic study soon won him the affection and loyalty of Safed's mystical community. After he died at the early age of 38, they preserved his teachings and transmitted them to later generations.

Luria's disciples referred to him as the Ari, an acronym for Adoneinu Rabbi Yitzhak ("Our Master Rabbi Isaac"). *Ari* is the Hebrew word meaning "lion," and indeed, the disciples of Rabbi Isaac considered him to be mighty as a lion in mystical knowledge.

Two Approaches to Judaism

Many talmudic scholars at first regarded the kabbalists as dangerous. The kabbalists, they said, did not show much interest in legal problems. Their way of life differed from the life of the scholars. As time went on, the conflict between these two approaches to Judaism diminished and Kabbalah became widely accepted. But in Safed, in the days of Rabbi Isaac Luria, they existed peacefully side-by-side.

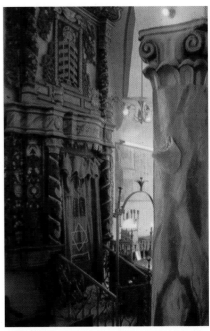

Interior of the Ari Synagogue in Safed, Israel.

The Shulhan Arukh

Rabbi Joseph Caro

Safed was also the home of Rabbi Joseph Caro (1488–1575). Born in Spain just a few years before the expulsion, Rabbi Joseph wandered through many lands before finding peace in Safed. In Turkey he had been the head of an academy of Jewish learning. After settling in Safed, he undertook a gigantic task: the compilation of an encyclopedic code of talmudic law that would be easier for Jews everywhere to use and follow than earlier legal codes and the original books of the Talmud.

A Handy Reference Book

Caro based his explication of Jewish law on the *Turim,* a code composed by Rabbi Jacob ben Asher (1270–1340) in Spain. He brought the *Turim* up to date by adding rabbinic decisions made in the two centuries since Jacob ben Asher and including Sephardic legal decisions and customs as currently enforced. For 30 years Joseph Caro worked on his commentary on the *Turim.* He then prepared a shorter, well-defined version in which he discussed every phase of Jewish life and all its rituals. Joseph Caro's code is called the *Shulhan Arukh* ("Prepared Table"). It proved a handy reference work for those seeking guidance on specific details of Jewish practice and custom. In spite of initial opposition among Ashkenazic rabbis, particularly in Poland, it finally won full recognition after the glosses of Rabbi Moses Isserles (1530–1572) were added to it.

The *Shulhan Arukh* was used by Jews in many lands. It was especially helpful in small communities where there was no scholar to turn to for guidance.

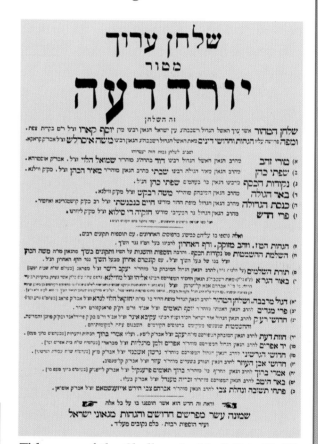

Title page of the *Shulhan Arukh*. It lists 20 different commentators. Included is the commentary by Moses Isserles.

Model of Rabbi Moses Isserles' Rema synagogue, Cracow, 1553 (Museum of the Diaspora, Tel Aviv).

False Messiahs

David Reubeni / 1490–1537

One day in the year 1524, a strange, dark man rode into the city of Rome on a white Arabian steed. Jews and Christians alike gaped in amazement and ran after him as he went to the palace of the pope for an audience. This man, who called himself David Reubeni, claimed to be the son of the king of the ancient Israelite tribe of Reuben. In a strange Hebrew dialect that was difficult for the Jews of Rome to understand, Reubeni told tales of the tribe of Reuben, deep in the lands of Arabia. Reubeni proposed a daring alliance to Pope Clement VII. If the pope would equip a Christian army to liberate Jerusalem and place him in command, Reubeni would muster the fighting men of the tribe of Reuben to join forces with it. Together they would free the Holy Land from the Ottoman yoke.

The pope was impressed by Reubeni. Times were difficult for the Catholic Church. The Reformation was taking hold in many lands and curbing the power of Rome. A new crusade that would take the Holy Land from the Turks seemed a worthwhile project. The pope arranged for Reubeni to visit the king of Portugal, who was expected to aid in this ambitious plan. In Portugal Reubeni was received with honor and the king gave serious consideration to his plan.

Solomon Molcho / 1500–1532

The Marranos of Portugal derived some benefit from Reubeni's arrival, for in his honor the Inquisition seems to have suspended its persecutions—a sign that its officials considered his mission authentic. Diego Pires, a prominent young Marrano, was deeply moved by Reubeni. Openly returning to Judaism, Diego left Portugal and went to Palestine to study the Kabbalah, changing his name to Solomon Molcho. In time he became convinced that he was meant to be a messenger of God on earth, sent to proclaim the coming of the Messiah. Solomon Molcho captured the imagination of many Jews, traveled to many lands, and finally appeared in Rome. There Molcho and Reubeni met. Reubeni, for reasons of his own, did not want to speak to Molcho, who was convinced of the righteousness of the cause he had embraced.

By this time, Charles V of Spain had decided that both men represented a danger since they were inciting both Christians and Jews to rebellion. Molcho was imprisoned by the Inquisition and put to death. Reubeni too seems to have died as a prisoner of the Inquisition.

The false Messiah David Reubeni, presented this letter to Pope Clement VII: "I am David, the son of King Solomon (may the memory of the righteous be blessed), and my brother is King Joseph, who is older than I, and who sits on the throne of his kingdom in the wilderness of Habor (Chaibar), and rules over thirty myriads of the tribe of Gad and of the tribe of Reuben and of the half-tribe of Manasseh. I have journeyed from before the king, my brother and his counselors, the seventy elders. They charged me to go first to Rome to the presence of the pope, may his glory be exalted."

David Molcho, another false Messiah, excited the imagination of Jews everywhere. Molcho's signature with a victory pennant.

The Netherlands

In the 15th and early 16th centuries, the Netherlands were under the dominion of Spain. The Protestant Dutch hated the Catholic Spaniards and their ways. Charles V, who ruled both Spain and the Holy Roman Empire, was determined to suppress any stirrings of revolt; he wanted his far-flung domains united in loyalty to church and crown, and therefore sought to crush Protestantism wherever he encountered it.

But Spanish rule could not maintain its grip on the freedom-loving Dutch. The people of the Netherlands fought Spain bitterly, and in 1581 declared their independence.

Meanwhile, Protestant England, also wary of Spain, was on the way to becoming a nation of seafarers, merchants, and colonists. Spain set out to conquer England, but in 1588, under Queen Elizabeth I, the English navy defeated and destroyed the Spanish Armada.

Marranos in Holland

After the Netherlands won their independence, large numbers of Marranos from Portugal and Spain fled to Amsterdam and Antwerp, where they reverted to their ancestral religion. The local Christians treated them with friendliness and tolerance, and before long major Sephardic communities had developed in the great trading cities of Holland and Belgium.

The Dutch Jerusalem

Throughout this era the city of Amsterdam was often called the Dutch Jerusalem, a name coined in 1596, when a group of Portuguese Marranos there returned to Judaism in a solemn public ceremony. From that time on, Amsterdam was one of the great centers of European Jewry. Jewish communities also grew up in the other cities of the Netherlands. Many Portuguese and Spanish Marranos became successful and respected traders in their new homeland and contributed to the growing power of the Netherlands.

Engraving by Adolf van der Laan (ca. 1710) showing the Portuguese synagogue on the left and the two Ashkenazic synagogues on the right in Amsterdam.

Jews in Germany

The Portuguese Marranos who settled in Amsterdam had trade connections with Jewish merchants in the German city of Hamburg. At first the Marranos in Hamburg were simply known as Portuguese, but after a time they openly professed their Judaism. Since they had become very useful to the merchant city, they were permitted to remain, although they had to accept the restrictions imposed on all Jews in Germany. Under the influence of the Portuguese immigrants, Hamburg became a center of active Jewish life.

Resolution of the Amsterdam Portuguese Jewish community granting pioneer Isaac da Costa a Sefer Torah for Curaçao in the West Indies, 1659. The Jews of Holland helped the new overseas communities in many ways.

Jews in the Dutch Colonies

Holland eventually gained a foothold in the New World, both in the West Indies and in Brazil, which was a Portuguese possession until the Dutch conquered it in 1631. There were many Marranos in Brazil, especially in the city of Recife. Under Dutch rule, they openly returned to the Jewish faith, dedicating a synagogue where they proudly worshipped in the Sephardic tradition and bringing a rabbi from Amsterdam to serve their community.

When Portugal began the reconquest of Brazil, the Jewish settlers fought side by side with their Dutch neighbors and many of them died in battle.

Rabbi Jacob Sasportas (1610–1698). In 1681 he was appointed Chacham in Amsterdam. He was a bitter opponent of Shabbatai Zevi.

Minute book, written in Portuguese, of the Spanish and Portuguese Jewish congregation in Amsterdam, 1656.

Rabbi Manasseh Ben Israel / 1604–1657

One of the most important rabbis in the Dutch Jerusalem was Manasseh Ben Israel. The son of Spanish Jews, he was steeped in Jewish learning. Many Christians in those days wanted to study the Bible in its original language rather than in translation, and they often turned to Manasseh Ben Israel for guidance.

Portrait of Rabbi Manasseh Ben Israel, painted by Rembrandt.

Letter from the Jews of London to Oliver Cromwell, dated March 24, 1655, pleading that "we may with security meet privately in our houses for our devotions."

Rembrandt the Painter

Among Rabbi Manasseh's many Christian friends was the great Dutch painter, Rembrandt van Rijn. Rembrandt was fascinated by the strong facial types and Mediterranean appearance of the Dutch Jews of Spanish and Portuguese descent, so different from the fair, northern Dutch. He asked many Jews to pose for him, among them Manasseh Ben Israel.

Manasseh was a student of the Kabbalah. Like many Jews of his day, he believed that the coming of the Messiah was near. A keen observer of political developments, he noted the great changes that had taken place in England since its break with Catholicism. In 1649, Oliver Cromwell and the Protestant Puritans had come into power and deposed the king. Many of England's political leaders looked to the Bible for inspiration. They seriously studied the workings of the Sanhedrin for guidance in conducting their own Parliament.

Manasseh Meets Cromwell

No Jews had lived openly or legally in England since the expulsion in 1290, but Manasseh Ben Israel felt the time for change was nigh. In 1655, after a difficult journey, he arrived in London and met with Cromwell. England's Protestant ruler was inclined to grant the rabbi's request, but many of his political associates were not so favorably disposed. As a result, the rabbi's plea was rejected. Still, his journey had not been wholly in vain. The following year a group of Marranos who were already living secretly in England returned to the religion of their ancestors and were granted the right to worship as they pleased. Eventually they were joined by other Jews, and Jewish communities arose again all over England.

Portrait of Oliver Cromwell.

Shabbatai Zevi / 1626–1673

As the 17th century progressed, messianic fervor spread among Jews everywhere, steadily intensifying because the kabbalists had calculated that 1648 was the year that would see the coming of the Messiah. Among those affected by the messianic yearning was Shabbatai Zevi, the son of refugees who had settled in the Turkish town of Smyrna (Izmir) after the expulsion from Spain. As a boy he studied the Kabbalah and became deeply involved in unraveling its intricate mysteries.

Shabbatai Zevi

Shabbatai the Messiah

In 1648, the year which was supposed to bring the Messiah, 22-year-old Shabbatai stood up in the synagogue of Smyrna and pronounced the Ineffable Name of God, something only permitted to the High Priest on the Day of Atonement. By this revolutionary act Shabbatai clearly declared himself to be the Messiah. The congregation was awed and stunned.

Shocked by what Shabbatai had done, the rabbi who had guided his studies excommunicated him. Shabbatai was forced to leave Smyrna. He had gained some loyal disciples, however, and accompanied by these followers, he set out for Jerusalem. After winning the support of the Jewish community of the Holy City, the group journeyed on to Cairo.

Even rabbis and scholars came under the spell of Shabbatai Zevi. New prayerbooks with prayers for Shabbatai as Messiah were printed in Amsterdam. Many Jews settled their affairs and prepared to leave for Palestine on Shabbatai's command. Even the Christian world watched attentively, for many Christians hoped that Shabbatai's messianic claims might be a portent of the eagerly awaited Second Coming of Christ.

Shabbatai and the Sultan

In 1666 the Ottoman sultan, concerned about the unrest spreading through his empire, had Shabbatai Zevi thrown in prison. He gave Shabbatai a choice between death and conversion to Islam. To everyone's amazement the would-be Messiah, who had sparked a fire of hope in Jewish hearts throughout the world, accepted conversion and became a Muslim!

Jewish communities everywhere were dumbfounded. Many found it impossible to believe that Shabbatai Zevi had really been nothing but an impostor, and many people, including some prominent scholars, continued to believe in him. Scholars and rabbis, who had disapproved of the Kabbalah even before Shabbatai Zevi's appearance, concentrated on the Talmud and urged the people to do likewise.

Title page of a Shabbatean prayerbook called *Tikkun*, printed in Amsterdam in 1666. It contains readings for each day and night of the year.

Baruch Spinoza / 1632–1677

Lens Grinder and Philosopher

Among the Jewish merchants and craftsmen in Amsterdam there were many brilliant and unusual people. Some were learned in the Talmud; others were immersed in the study of the Kabbalah. One of them was Baruch (Benedict) Spinoza (1632–1677). The son of refugees from Spain, Spinoza had studied the Torah and the Talmud like all the other Jewish boys of his day. He had also studied not only the great philosophers of Judaism but the secular works of the philosophers of ancient Greece and Rome. Spinoza was a brilliant young man, and his teachers, the rabbis of Amsterdam, hoped he would become their brightest disciple and successor.

Baruch Spinoza (1632–1677) was a Jewish philosopher. In 1656 he was excommunicated for his shocking ideas.

But Spinoza gradually isolated himself from Jewish life. He did not follow all the laws of the *Shulhan Arukh,* and some of his ideas seemed shocking and sacrilegious. Spinoza wrote brilliant philosophical works in which he stated that God was present in all things and that humans could serve Him by being just and righteous to one another.

Spinoza also rejected the divine origin of the Torah, and that was considered shocking by the Jewish community of the 17th century. Spinoza's ideas seemed to threaten Jewish unity and survival. Hence he had to be rejected.

Spinoza Is Excommunicated

In 1656 the rabbis of Amsterdam excommunicated Spinoza, and as a result he was regarded as an outsider by the official Jewish community.

Spinoza earned his living by making lenses for spectacles. He liked this work, and after his excommunication he took his tools and moved to the little village of Rijnsberg on the outskirts of Amsterdam. Here he lived quietly, devoted to his studies and writings. Many of the great scholars of the time came to visit the humble lens grinder. He died at the age of 45, a lonely man. In later years Spinoza came to be universally recognized as one of the greatest philosophic minds.

Spinoza's house in The Hague. The plaque records that he lived there from 1671 to 1677.

Moses Hayim Luzzatto / 1707–1747

A Poet and Mystic

Another unusual personality who caused a stir in the Jewish community of Amsterdam, some years later, was the poet and mystic Moses Hayim Luzzatto (1707–1747). Like Spinoza, he too earned his livelihood as a lens grinder. Born in the Italian city of Padua, Luzzatto made a name for himself by the age of 20 with a book of poetry patterned on the biblical psalms. Inspired by the spirit of the Renaissance, he wrote plays on biblical themes that had a lasting influence on the development of modern Hebrew literature. As he grew older, Luzzatto turned more and more to Kabbalah and the Zohar.

The Kabbalah Forbidden

In Luzzatto's time, the rabbis of Italy forbade young Jewish scholars to study the Kabbalah, because they felt that only mature men would be able to do so without falling victim to confusion and doubt. The rabbis strongly disapproved of Luzzatto's interest in mysticism. They were shocked when the poet ignored their warnings and wrote a book which he entitled *The Second Zohar*. As a result Luzzatto was compelled to leave Italy in 1733. He went to Amsterdam to begin a new life, grinding lenses for a living, but here too he was not able to write works on Kabbalah.

Luzzatto in Israel

As Luzzatto grew older he began to see the Holy Land as his salvation, as the place in which he could pursue his kabbalistic studies, and write in peace. He and his family managed to translate their yearning into reality and, after an arduous journey, settled in Tiberias. Unfortunately, soon

Besides his psalms, poems, and plays, Luzzatto also wrote a book on Jewish ethics called *The Way of the Righteous* (*Mesillat Yesharim*). This much-studied book has become a classic and has been translated into several languages.

after their arrival the entire family was wiped out by an epidemic of plague that ravaged the country.

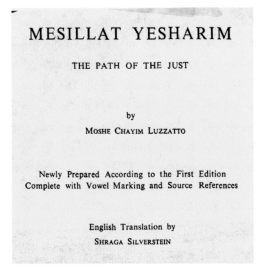

Title page of the English edition of *Mesillat Yesharim*.

In Eastern Europe

Early Russian Beginnings

According to some traditions, the first Jews to settle in areas that later became part of the Russian Empire arrived there after the destruction of the Temple in 586 B.C.E. They were brought to these regions when Nebuchadnezzar of Babylon deported large numbers of Jews to territories in Armenia, the Caucasus region, and along the shores of the Black Sea.

A sprinkling of Jewish settlers settled in Eastern Europe in Roman times, when Jewish traders traveled along the great rivers and brought their wares to many distant lands. Others moved into Russia from Persia and Arabia. Around 800 C.E., some the Khazars, a Turkic people who lived beyond the Black Sea, converted to Judaism. It is possible that only the royal family, and some of the nobility converted. They continued to practice the Jewish religion until the mid-10th century, when the Russians overran their kingdom.

Beginnings of Polish Jewry

Most of the Jews of Eastern Europe, however, came from Germany. Toward the end of the Middle Ages, they began wandering eastward to Poland, which at that time included Ukraine and Lithuania, in order to escape persecution in the cities and towns of Germany. The Polish kings eagerly welcomed them, for there were many merchants and artisans among the Jewish migrants, and Poland badly needed their commercial and technical expertise.

The populace of Poland at the time consisted of two classes—nobles who owned the land and peasants who worked it; there was virtually no middle class. The kings of Poland hoped that the newcomers would build cities and bring commerce and industry to their realm. To encourage the Jewish immigrants, they made them directly subordinate to the crown rather than to the nobles in the regions where they settled. This gave the Jewish settlers a special legal status that protected them from many manifestations of anti-Semitism and enabled them to live under their own laws.

Drawn by the opportunities Poland offered, ever greater numbers of Jews moved eastward. As cities grew, Jewish communities sprang up. In time, large and prospering Jewish communities flourished in Warsaw, Vilna, Lublin, Posen (Poznan), and Cracow, as well as many smaller towns.

The Old-New Synagogue (Altneuschul) in Prague, built in the late 13th or early 14th century, in the heart of the Jewish quarter. Brick gables were added in the 15th cent.

A Russian cavalryman

King Casimir the Great

The charter granted to the first Jewish settlers was renewed by King Casimir the Great, who reigned from 1333 to 1370. Casimir was renowned for building many new cities, and was often referred to as king of the serfs and the Jews, for he was a very tolerant ruler who was genuinely concerned about the welfare of the serfs and his Jewish subjects.

With the arrival of so many skilled immigrants, Poland experienced an era of rapid progress and development. Many non-Jews joined the movement eastward, and unfortunately they brought to their new homes not only their skills but also their traditional prejudices. They were eager to restrict their Jewish neighbors, whom they regarded as rivals, just as they had done in Germany, and often found allies in the church. But Poland's kings defended the Jews, and for some 300 years Polish Jewry enjoyed an era of peace and freedom.

The Jews as Assets

The Jews proved to be an asset to Poland. They set up a banking system and printed Poland's first paper money. Some of these early banknotes bear the names of the Polish kings of the time printed in Hebrew letters.

Many Jews in Poland were employed as managers of estates, tax collectors, and financial advisors to the nobility, and the

A model of a wooden synagogue built about 1600.

nobles valued their services. Jews were also active in the export of grain, salt, timber, and other natural resources, and imported goods needed from abroad. In addition, they owned and operated many of the country's inns, taverns, and stores, were active in transporting merchandise from place to place, and played a major role in many of the skilled crafts so essential to a pre-industrial economy.

Stately house in Lvov, of Simha Menahem, Jewish physician to King John III Sobieski of Poland.

Polish coins with Hebrew inscriptions.

The Jews of Poland

The Kahal

The Jews of Poland constituted a separate social class distinct from the four "estates" of medieval society. They were neither nobles nor peasants, nor city-dwelling burghers like the Christian merchants and artisans. And, of course, they did not belong to the clergy. In recognition of their status, King Sigismund Augustus issued a charter in 1551 that guaranteed the Jews of Poland the right to govern themselves.

The Jews of the four provinces ruled by the Polish kings—Greater Poland, Little Poland, Volhynia, and Lemberg—were organized into self-governing communities headed by a Kahal (assembly) known as the Va'ad Arba Aratzot (Council of the Four Lands), whose members were the elected representatives of Poland's many Jewish communities.

The Council of Four Lands

Whereas the Jews of ancient Babylonia had been ruled by an individual, the exilarch, Polish Jewry was ruled by an elected council. The Va'ad Arba Aratzot negotiated with the king's representatives and collected the taxes levied on the country's Jews. It enforced the law in the Jewish communities and was in charge of Jewish courts, schools, trade guilds, and communal char-

The Jewish community enjoyed a self-sufficient economy and had its own merchants, farmers, and tradesmen. These paintings by Arthur Szyk picture a Jewish blacksmith and baker at work.

ities. When necessary, it appointed a spokesman or advocate (shtadlan) to represent it in dealings with Christian officials.

Although the Jews of Poland were only allowed to live in certain areas, they managed to build up an active and independent communal life. They had their own bankers and merchants, farmers and laborers, and their own craft guilds of butchers, bakers, printers, and locksmiths.

The Yiddish Language

Gradually, the Jews of Poland evolved a language of their own. In medieval Germany their ancestors had spoken German with a significant admixture of Hebrew. The migrants from Germany who settled in Poland continued speaking this language in their new homeland. Over time Polish words and expressions were added. The language that evolved from these developments is known as Yiddish.

The Yiddish language, written in Hebrew letters but ultimately derived from medieval German, soon came to be the main form of intercommunication among the Jews of Eastern Europe. By 1700,

Meeting place of the Council of the Four Lands, Lublin, 16th and 17th cent.

Yiddish was playing an important role in religious, intellectual, literary, and personal correspondence. In some quarters, in the 18th and 19th centuries, especially among those who opposed Zionism and the use of Hebrew for secular purposes, Yiddish came to be regarded as the Jewish national language.

Jewish Education

The Jewish communities of Eastern Europe organized their own school systems. Boys from 4 to 13 years of age attended the heder (elementary school). The better students went on to the yeshiva for advanced studies. Many communities had more than one yeshiva, each headed by a learned rabbi. Great care was taken to provide boys with a thorough Jewish education. Those who had neither time, money, nor aptitude for advanced learning became workers, craftsmen, or businessmen.

Rabbi Moses Isserles

As we have already learned, Rabbi Joseph Caro's *Shulhan Arukh* gained universal acceptance among Sephardic Jews. However, it lacked information on the customs and modes of observance evolved by the Ashkenazim. Rabbi Moses Isserles, a saintly scholar who lived in Cracow, remedied this lack by compiling all the decisions handed down by Ashkenazic rabbis and scholars into a supplement to the *Shulhan Arukh*. Since the title of Caro's work means "The Prepared Table," Isserles called his supplement the *Mappah*, or "Tablecloth." With this addition the *Shulhan Arukh* was accepted by Jews everywhere.

The four volumes of the *Shulhan Arukh* are very detailed. In the years that followed, to make its laws more accessible to general readers, several scholars edited popular, easy-to-understand abridgements of the text. One of the most popular of these is the *Kitzur* ("Short") *Shulhan Arukh*, published by Rabbi Solomon Ganzfried in 1864. It has been translated into many languages.

The Jews in this Polish synagogue are wearing fur hats called streimels that were worn on holidays and special occasions. This rabbi and his disciples are praying in front of a desk called a shtender. The texts are located in shelves above them. The Yiddish word for "standing" is *shtayt*, hence the Yiddish word *shtender*.

English tranlation of the *Kitzur Shulhan Arukh*.

Revolt and War

Russian Unrest

The 17th century was a time of unrest all over Europe. There were conflicts between Catholics and Protestants, and between members of different Protestant denominations. In the social-political sphere, the revived interest in learning, coupled with the spirit of the Reformation, gave rise to new ideas and new demands. The burghers of the cities wanted more freedom. The serfs—the poor, dependent peasants—developed a sense of self-respect and struggled to break loose from the bondage in which they were held by the nobility.

The peasants of Ukraine hated their Polish overlords. They were members of the Orthodox Church, whereas the Poles were Roman Catholics. The unfortunate Jews were caught in the middle, especially because most of the contact the peasants had with their masters was through Jewish tax-collectors and estate managers. Thus, the Jew was identified with the hated landlord. When the Ukrainians revolted, they launched their first attacks against the Jews.

The Cossacks Spread Destruction

The Ukrainian uprising was spearheaded by fierce peasant-soldiers known as Cossacks. Their commander, Bogdan Chmielnicki, led his troops against the hated Polish landlords and the Jews of Ukraine and Poland. Very often, the terrified Poles abandoned the Jews and left them to their fate. Although the isolated Jewish communities took up arms and bravely tried to defend themselves, many thousands of Jews were killed within a few months. Even in the few instances where Poles and Jews united in defense of their towns, it was to no avail, for the Cossacks swept through the land like a wild hurricane, spreading death and destruction wherever they struck.

In the town of Nemirov, on June 10, 1648, the Cossacks, with the collaboration of the Poles, massacred more than 6,000 Jewish men, women, and children. Similar scenes occurred in many other towns.

Expulsion from the Ukraine

The king of Poland, in order to make peace with Chmielnicki, named him prince of Ukraine. As a condition of this deal, Chmielnicki stipulated that the Jews were to be expelled from Ukraine. But peace did not come to the torn country even then, for the Cossacks were still not satisfied. They received aid from hordes of Russians who rode through the land, leaving death and ruin in their wake.

The Cossack leader, Bogdan Chmielnicki, killed thousands of Ukrainian Jews in the revolt he led in 1648.

By the time the Cossacks and the Poles finally signed a peace treaty in 1654, 700 Jewish communities had been destroyed and more than 100,000 Jews killed. The Council of the Four Lands had disintegrated. The surviving Jews were left impoverished and scattered.

To make things worse, the Orthodox Church increased its hostility toward the Jews, accusing them of meddling in its affairs. Blood-libel accusations fanned by the church began to spread in which the Jews were accused of using the blood of Christian children in making matzot for Passover. Anti-Jewish riots terrorized the Jews in eastern Poland.

In order to obtain a feeling of hope that conditions would someday improve, many Jews turned to the Kabbalah. According to the calculations of the kabbalists, the time was ripe for the Messiah to appear and put an end to war and hatred. As a result, many Jews were easily swayed by the messianic claims of Shabbatai Zevi and his followers.

A street in Lublin, a major economic center for the Jews of Poland from the 16th cent. Lublin also became a center for the study of Torah, and was nicknamed Jerusalem of Poland.

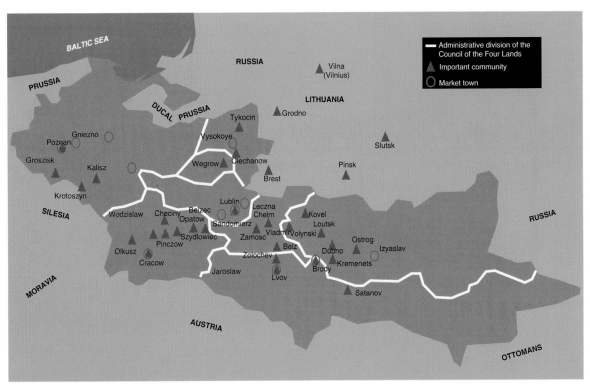

The territory administered by the Council of Four Lands. The area was divided into districts to simplify its administration.

Pale of Settlement

The last half of the 18th century was another stormy era both for Poland and for its Jews. Three times the land was invaded and partitioned by its more powerful neighbors. By 1796 nothing remained and Poland lost its independence altogether. Depending on where they lived, the Jews of Poland now became subjects of either Russia, Prussia, or Austria. To further compound their difficulties, even before the partitions Poland's last king, Stanislaw II Poniatowski, had abolished their two institutions of self-government, the Council of the Four Lands and the Council of Lithuania.

Several hundred wooden synagogues were built in Poland during the 17th and 18th cent. Unfortunately they were vulnerable to arson, and almost none remain.

Stanislaw II Poniatowski, the last king of Poland.

Catherine the Great

The ruler of Russia at this time, Catherine the Great, regarded herself as a progressive and liberal empress, but her subjects lived under extremely primitive conditions. Russia had a wealthy nobility and a merchant class composed of immigrants from Germany. The rest of the people were mostly serfs. The partitions of Poland brought Catherine the lion's share of Polish Jewry. In order to prevent this mass of Jews

from expanding into other parts of the Russian Empire, she and her successors restricted their right of residence to the areas taken from Poland in which they were already living.

Life in the Pale

The Pale of Settlement, the area in the Russian government allowed Jews to live, included eastern Poland, Ukraine, and Lithuania. In addition to its Jewish residents, it had a much larger population of Christians, many of whom were quite hostile to their Jewish neighbors.

Catherine the Great was the daughter of a minor German ruler. In 1745 she married the Russian Tsar Peter III and soon after his mysterious death, in 1761, made herself the ruler of the greatest state in Europe. Domestically, she ruled with an iron hand and militarily advanced Russian power. She acquired Lithuania and the Ukraine from the Polish kingdom, and the Black Sea territories from the Ottoman empire. Envious statesmen saw Catherine's success as the work of the Devil.

It was here, in the little towns and villages of the Pale, in a few crowded cities and lonely inns along the highway, that most of Europe's Jews were to live for the next 200 years. Many harsh restrictions were placed upon them: they had to pay high taxes and could not move or travel without permission; they did not attend Russian schools or academies of higher learning and were barred from many other public institutions. Nonetheless, Jewish life in the Pale was active and full. While all but a few of the Russian nobles were illiterate, even the humblest Jewish family sent its sons to the heder to learn to read and write and engage in studying the Torah. The very restrictions that had been forced upon them served to unite the Jews of the Pale to a way of life based on brotherhood, neighborliness, and genuine affection for one another.

Ukrainian woodcutters drink in a Jewish-owned tavern. Note the costumes of the Jews. Painted in 1870 in Poland, by F. Lewicki.

Jewish Life in Poland

After the Chmielnicki revolt, the Cossack wars, and the general disillusion that set in after the exposure of Shabbatai Zevi and his false messianic claims, Jewish life in Poland went into a decline. The institutions of self-government were abolished. Many thriving communities disappeared; others were greatly reduced in size. Many communities could not even maintain their school systems.

Despite these serious problems, and the accompanying demoralization, this period was to produce two great religious leaders, each quite different from the other and each concerned with a different way of life. One was Israel ben Eliezer, known as the Baal Shem Tov; the other was Elijah ben Solomon, the Gaon of Vilna.

The Russian general Roumantsov leading his troops to victory over the Turks, August 1, 1770

The Baal Shem Tov / 1700–1760

Israel ben Eliezer

Israel ben Eliezer was born in a small town in Ukraine about 1698. When still a small child he lost both his parents and was cared for by the community. After graduating from the heder he became the assistant to his teacher. Israel liked children, and they, in turn, loved to listen to his stories. Although he was not known as a talmudic scholar, Israel was a bright young man with a charismatic manner and mystical disposition. He was also known as a healer and wonder-worker.

Israel married a young woman called Anna. From contemporary Polish records it appears that the two were given a house in Mezhbozh by the community, along with a small stipend.

The Worship of the Heart

All around him Israel could behold the beauty God had created. The humble lime digger was convinced that the holiness, or Shekhinah, of God dwelt within every living thing. All human beings, he believed, had the ability to see and experience the Shekhinah within themselves and around themselves. Everyone, scholar and simple laborer alike, he asserted, could reach spiritual heights by prayer and communing with God. The "worship of the heart" through joy and ecstasy, he taught, is of greater importance than dry, routine, ritual observance. Israel infused religious zest and vigor into the hearts of the physically downtrodden and spiritually impoverished masses.

Israel learned to make healing salves and ointments from plants and herbs, for he wanted to help the sick and the suffering. He also kept an inn which his wife managed while he devoted himself to teaching and healing. Faithful and inspired students flocked to him.

Day of Atonement in a Shtetl Synagogue. **Oil painting by Maurycy Gottlieb, 1878.**

Israel's Teachings

Israel ben Eliezer's teachings appealed not only to students but also, in the next generation, to the humble classes of the Jewish community.

He wrote no books; his wisdom was spread by word of mouth among rabbis and among the tradesmen, artisans, and laborers who were his followers. His followers told one another many wonderful stories about the wondrous deeds he performed, and before long the kindly Israel ben Eliezer was known as the Baal Shem Tov, the Master of the Good (Holy) Name, for it was said that he could heal people by wearing amulets. He is also known as the Besht, an acronym made up of the first letters of Baal Shem Tov.

Hasid and his wife in holiday dress.

The Hasidim

The followers of the Baal Shem Tov, who called themselves Hasidim ("pious ones") would dance with joy in their synagogues when they welcomed the Sabbath. Even in the midst of fervent prayers they would dance and sing niggunim, wordless melodies in praise of God. The leaders of the Hasidim in the generations after the Baal Shem Tov were known as Tzaddikim ("righteous ones"), and their disciples followed them with great fervor. As time passed, some of the Tzaddikim became men of great power and influence.

The synagogue of the Baal Shem Tov.

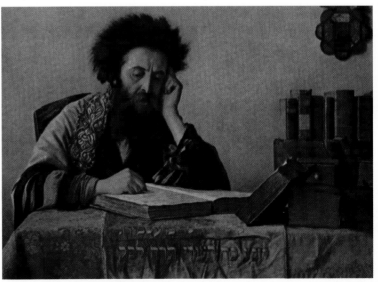

Hasidic scholar wearing a *streimel*. A *streimel* is a fox fur hat worn by some Hasidic sects on holidays and special ocasions

The Gaon of Vilna / 1720–1797

Elijah ben Solomon

The rabbis who fought against Hasidism were called Mitnagdim ("opponents"). Their leader was the Vilna Gaon—Elijah ben Solomon (1720–1797), the greatest among the many scholars of Vilna, a city known as the Jerusalem of Lithuania because of the great schools that flourished there. Elijah never accepted an official position as rabbi. He spent many hours in his quiet study at scholarly work, and, on occasion, teaching a small circle of disciples—advanced scholars who wanted to acquire his approach to talmudic study. His method was one of exacting detail. He would first study each passage thoroughly, and then refer to its original sources in the Mishnah and in the Torah itself. This thorough method made for a much clearer understanding of the Law.

Like the great scholars of earlier days, the Vilna Gaon studied mathematics and astronomy in addition to the works of Jewish mysticism. A few of his disciples encouraged the study of the sciences as essential for a proper understanding of Torah. This was unusual, for in those days most yeshiva scholars confined themselves strictly to teaching the Babylonian Talmud and the commentaries of Rashi and the tosafists.

The Vilna Gaon never held public office. Unofficially, however, he was the acknowledged spiritual leader of Lithuanian Jewry.

Conflict Between Hasidim and Mitnagdim

In the days of the Vilna Gaon the conflict between Hasidim and Mitnagdim became very bitter. The Tzaddikim had become very powerful, for their followers had come to regard them as intermediaries between the ordinary Hasid and God. The Mitnagdim, on the other hand, maintained that all human beings were personally responsible to God and therefore no intermediary was needed.

The Vilna Gaon took up the fight against Hasidism, going so far as to excommunicate its leaders and forbidding his followers to intermarry with its adherents. In time, however, this ban was lifted. As it became evident that the Hasidic faith fully followed the laws and commandments of the Talmud and the *Shulhan Arukh,* the two ways of Judaism made peace with one another. Hasidim and Mitnagdim still persisted in their different ways, as they do to the present time, but each group came to respect the other and to have a sense of appreciation for its contributions to Judaism.

The Vilna Gaon

New Horizons

First Stirrings of Democracy

During the 18th century more tolerant ideas first advanced in the Renaissance took on new life. Europe was slowly outgrowing the idea of absolute monarchy in which a king ruled supreme and an aristocracy had the right to subject the rest of the people. A new class of citizens had arisen—burghers who lived in the cities. Many of them were merchants, who helped build connections with other countries and with the faraway colonies of the New World. Also among the burghers were doctors and teachers. Universities began to rise in the cities of Europe, attended by the sons of nobles and wealthy burghers. Writers and poets put forth new and stimulating ideas.

The Reformation had stimulated widespread interest in the Bible, and many Christians had become aware that the Hebrew Scriptures were part of their religious heritage. Despite this, the Jews, whose ancestors had given gave the Bible to the world, were among the most despised people in Europe.

The Court Jews

Occasionally an individual Jew would rise to a position of high honor. At many a European royal court, especially in the many princedoms of Germany, a Jewish banker, often referred to as a court Jew, managed the sovereign's financial and business affairs. The court Jew usually enjoyed respect and prestige, but his position was precarious, for in many instances the kindness of the prince would turn to wrath.

Frequently a court Jew would speak to his prince on behalf of his community. Sometimes Jewish merchants who had helped a free city in time of war would be

The old synagogue in Berlin.

invited to settle there with their families and friends. In this way some Jewish communities increased in size. But there also were small communities surrounded by the high walls of the ghetto from which a Jew could go forth only when he had to do business. No social relations existed between the world outside and the ghetto Jews.

Developments outside the ghetto were foreign to the Jews of the 17th and 18th centuries, except insofar as they affected their lives directly in the form of persecution or war. So isolated was the life of the Jews in Germany that their spoken language was not the German of everyone else but Judeo-German, medieval German closely interwoven with Hebrew words, the same dialect that in Eastern Europe had evolved into Yiddish.

The writers and thinkers of Germany had little occasion to meet Jews. But as they became interested in the theories of human equality and natural rights, they began to turn their attention to the minority that suffered so much discrimination in their own country.

Moses Mendelssohn / *1729–1786*

Moses Mendelssohn was a small man who spoke with a slight stammer, but he had a dynamic spirit and a brilliant mind. The son of a Torah scribe, Mendelssohn was born in the German town of Dessau and studied with a rabbi there. When he was a boy of 14 his beloved teacher moved to Berlin. The boy followed him, and on paying the tax required of Jews, he succeeded in gaining admission to the city.

Moses Mendelssohn

Mendelssohn Finds a New World

Mendelssohn found a new world in Berlin. Even though most of the city's Jews lived much as their brethren did in other German communities, there were quite a few enterprising Jewish merchants and financiers in Berlin who enjoyed special privileges and were in contact with the world outside the ghetto. Young Mendelssohn continued his Jewish studies with his mentor, but broadened his education by taking up a variety of other subjects as well. He found willing teachers with whom he studied the writings of the philosophers.

Mendelssohn secured employment as tutor to the children of a wealthy silk manufacturer. In his spare time he began to write on philosophy and current issues, expounding his ideas in a pure, flowing German. Moses Mendelssohn was the first German Jew of his day whose writings and intellectual interests transcended the ghetto walls. Berlin's intellectual and cul-

Title page of Book of Psalms, translated into German by Moses Mendelssohn.

tural elite became very much interested in this unusual man.

Difficulties in Germany

All through the German lands Jews were still confined to ghettos. In the great and ancient communities of Frankfurt, Mayence, Worms, and Hamburg, as well as in the new community of Berlin, they lived under severe restrictions. Usually only the eldest son of a Jewish family was permitted to marry, and then only after paying a special tax. Jews also had to pay taxes for such acts as entering a walled city. Often families would be separated by these cruel restrictions, because their daughters and sons had to go to distant communities to marry and have families of their own.

It was difficult for Jews to earn a living, for most of them were only permitted to engage in small-scale businesses like moneylending and dealing in second-hand goods. They were not allowed to own land or real estate outside the crowded ghettos.

A Protected Jew

Moses Mendelssohn became a privileged, or "protected," Jew—a status normally reserved for the most important Jewish merchants and financiers, and for a few Jewish physicians who treated influential non-Jewish patients. Thanks to the freedom provided by this status, Mendelssohn met many of the writers and scholars of the day. He even met Frederick the Great, the king of Prussia, who was very much interested in philosophy and the arts.

Mendelssohn's main concern, however, was the Jewish community. Convinced that German Jewry had to break down the ghetto walls and participate in the life outside, he devoted himself to the task of bringing his brethren the modern learning and culture that would make this possible. Mendelssohn knew that to participate fully in life outside the ghetto the German Jews would first have to learn the German language. He had no intention of sacrificing Jewish education, however, and participated in publishing a magazine that carried articles, poems, and commentaries in Hebrew. But he insisted that in addition to traditional Jewish studies, Jews must learn German and become acquainted with the world around them.

At that time few German children went to school. Most of the common people were illiterate. But the Jews all knew how to read and write in Hebrew. Under Mendelssohn's influence, new schools were founded in Berlin where Jewish children were given their Jewish and secular education under one roof. He insisted, too, that the children receive trade and vocational training to prepare them for life as free citizens among their non-Jewish neighbors.

The First German Torah Translation

Facility in German, Mendelssohn felt, was essential. Few German Jews knew the language well, and virtually none could read it. To provide them with a learning resource, Mendelssohn translated the Five Books of Moses into German. He had it printed in Hebrew characters, however, so that Jews could read it even if they did not know the German alphabet. The translation appeared with a Hebrew commentary prepared by Mendelssohn in collaboration with a biblical scholar.

The new translation was published with the permission of the rabbis of Germany, and at first it was widely accepted. Since most Jews already knew and had read the Bible in Hebrew, the translation satisfied an important need. It became a learning tool for everyone who wanted to learn German; copies found their way even to the Yiddish-speaking villages of far-off Russia where isolated students sought to master German as the first step on the road to enlightened self-improvement.

Before long, however, the rabbis decided that Mendelssohn's German Bible and modern commentary were dangerous innovations; the old, traditional way of teaching was safer and more desirable. This did not deter those who were eager to learn German from continuing to rely on Mendelssohn's Bible.

Moses Mendelssohn playing chess.

Edict of Frederick the Great with regard to the conversion of Jews.

Edict of Tolerance / 1782

No explicit laws to better the lot of the Jews were passed in the German states during Mendelssohn's lifetime. But new ideas had paved a path for new hopes and attitudes.

Wilhelm Dohm

Among Mendelssohn's many Christian friends who were favorably disposed toward the new concepts of liberty and tolerance was Christian Wilhelm Dohm, a Prussian lawyer. When the Jews of Alsace asked Mendelssohn to write a petition requesting the authorities to remove some of the heavy restrictions placed upon them, it was to Dohm that Mendelssohn turned, asking him to draft the text of the memorandum. Dohm not only complied with his friend's request, but also wrote a plea for freedom and equality for all the Jews of Western Europe.

Dohm's plea brought Joseph II, the emperor of Austria, to proclaim the famous Edict of Tolerance (1782). While this law did not lift all restrictions from the Jews of Austria, it eased their burden considerably and opened doors hitherto closed to them. They no longer had to pay special poll taxes and wear the yellow badge; they were allowed to engage in trade and manufacturing and to become apprenticed to Christian master craftsmen. However, when Joseph died in 1790, most of the restrictions were revived.

Other Proclamations of Freedom

Meanwhile, in the New World across the ocean, the American colonies had revolted against England. Their Declaration of Independence and Constitution stimulated much discussion among thinking people throughout Europe. The laws of the new land incorporated many of the same ideas that Mendelssohn and his friends had helped formulate in Berlin.

Freedom and Assimilation

Moses Mendelssohn fought not only for enlightenment and religious freedom but also to ensure the survival of Judaism and its traditions. He was by no means an assimilationist. He did not want the Jewish people to merge into the other nations of the world and lose its distinctive identity. His goal was to enable his brethren to make a contribution to civilization outside the ghetto and to live in peace and harmony side by side with their Gentile neighbors.

Medal commemorating Joseph II's Edict of Tolerance, Vienna, 1782.

Revolution and Reform

The French Revolution / 1789

For a hundred years France had set the trends in Europe. In Germany, Poland, and Austria, and even in Russia, French was the language of the nobility, the educated, and the wealthy. French ideas and styles were adopted and imitated.

When French philosophers, writers, and poets first began to speak out for religious and political freedom, the rulers of France were greatly disturbed, for they needed obedient subjects who would willingly supply the immense sums of money necessary to support the elegant French court and powerful French army.

On July 14, 1789, the people of Paris stormed the Bastille, a fortress in which many of those who had been unable to pay the high taxes were imprisoned. This was the start of the French Revolution, an upheaval in which the people came to power.

In 1789, the year the Revolution began, the French Assembly proclaimed the Declaration of the Rights of Man. This document, which is similar to the American Declaration of Independence, declared that all human beings are born free and entitled to equal rights.

In 1790, the Jews of Bordeaux were granted equality. A decree passed in 1791 gave all French Jews the rights and privileges of full citizenship. But then the new French republic became involved in war. First, it had to defend itself against the monarchs of Europe, who were afraid that the spirit of revolt would spread to their lands.

A short time later, the French armies themselves became armies of conquest. They were led by a young general named Napoleon Bonaparte.

The Reign of Napoleon

Napoleon was a brilliant strategist. A highly ambitious man, he had dreams of great conquest. He hoped to carry the ideals and the new freedom of the young republic of France to every country in Europe.

Wherever his conquering armies took over, serfs and Jews were freed. The ghetto walls of Germany, Austria, and Italy fell. Many Europeans regarded Napoleon as a great liberator. The laws he promulgated, known as the Napoleonic Code, lent legal force to the concepts of freedom and civil liberties. His ambition was to be the undisputed ruler of the French state, the crowned conqueror of Europe. In 1804 he became emperor of France.

In 1806 Napoleon convened an assembly of Jewish notables and announced that Jews were now officially citizens of the French nation. The emperor is shown raising the Jewess while the rabbis kneel at his feet.

Freedom and Citizenship

Napoleon Convenes a Sanhedrin

Eager to gain the loyalty of the Jews and also to exercise a measure of control over them, Napoleon convened an assembly patterned on the ancient Sanhedrin. Altogether, 71 representatives, 46 rabbis and 25 laymen, were chosen to settle legal and religious questions and to demonstrate loyalty to Napoleon's France.

The Sanhedrin was soon dissolved, but it served to emphasize some of the fundamentals of Judaism to the non-Jewish world.

Napoleon Bonaparte

Reaction

Eventually the allied countries of Europe defeated Napoleon. With Napoleon defeated and banished, the Jews lost many of the freedoms he had granted them. In some parts of Germany and Austria they had to return to the ghettos, and the peasants were forced to revert to serfdom.

Having had a taste of freedom, the Jews found it difficult to readjust to the old restrictions. Some German and Austrian Jews had attended universities and embarked upon brilliant careers; they were now respected bankers and merchants, or high-ranking government officials. Some of them, concluding that there were many advantages to be gained from converting to Christianity, underwent baptism in order to be able to keep their positions.

Changes Within

Most of the Jews of Germany and Austria continued to follow the ways of their ancestors. But, like everyone in the 19th century, they, too, had to adjust to the radical changes that were occurring in their time.

Patriotism and nationalism reached new heights. The Jews were proud of their newly won rights of citizenship in the countries in which they lived. And this brought them face to face with a new problem: how to remain faithful to the traditions of Judaism and still be loyal, active citizens of the countries that had accorded them freedom and equality.

Impelled by a desire to eliminate the differences between themselves and those in whose midst they lived, many Jews were anxious to change Judaism itself.

Napoleon became the ruler of France after the turmoil of the French Revolution. During his regime France conquered much of Europe. In 1821 he died in exile on the tiny island of St. Helena.

Changes and Resistance in Germany

Reform Judaism

Those calling for radical changes in Judaism founded the Reform movement. They felt that if Judaism was to have a meaningful function in the modern world, it was necessary to eliminate old ceremonies and ideas which seemed antiquated or inappropriate, or which reflected the sensibility of the narrow life of the medieval ghetto.

Rabbi Zechariah Frankel

One of the leaders of this new movement, headed by Rabbi Abraham Geiger (1810–1874), proposed a different form of service. They introduced sermons and prayers in German, the everyday language of the people, and shortened Hebrew prayers that seemed too long. References to the return to Zion and the coming of the Messiah were omitted. Believing that a "reformed" Judaism would adjust Jewish life to the demands of the times, they set aside the authority of the Talmud and the *Shulhan Arukh.* The Reform movement took root in some of the larger German cities and the first Reform temple was dedicated in Hamburg.

Orthodoxy

Many Jews steadfastly resisted the changes proposed by the reformers, maintaining that any break in the chain of tradition would endanger the very foundations of Judaism. Their approach is now known as Orthodox Judaism. The most influential early opponent of reform was Rabbi Moses Schreiber (1763–1839), who was born in Germany and later became known as the Chatam Sofer, after the title of many of his works. From his position as rabbi in Pressburg, Hungary, he rallied traditional-ist-minded Jews against any changes in the synagogue service. Orthodoxy, which held the loyalty of most German Jews, had a number of brilliant spokesmen. In the next generation, the most prominent among them was Rabbi Samson Raphael Hirsch (1808–1888). Hirsch was convinced that Jews could be good citizens, steeped in the culture and learning of their country, and still remain loyal to the laws that had come down through the ages in the Bible and Talmud.

The Historical School

A third group took a midway position between Reform and Orthodoxy. Led by Zechariah Frankel (1801–1875), the president of the rabbinical seminary in Breslau (Wroclaw), this movement was known as the Historical School, and eventually became what is today called Conservative Judaism. It emphasized the importance of the historical continuity of the Jewish heritage. The adherents of the Historical School knew that change was inevitable and acknowledged that Judaism had undergone changes throughout its history, but they insisted that innovations had to be within the framework of Jewish tradition. Radical reform, they felt, was not in keeping with the evolving spirit of Judaism.

Kriegs-Hagadah 1914–1915

הגדה של פסח

A German army War Haggadah used during World War I.

Judaism and Civil Liberties

The "Science of Judaism"

A group of young German Jewish university graduates believed that the best way to ensure the survival of Judaism was to make its history and values better known. To this end, they began to apply the same analytical methods to the study of the Jewish heritage that were used in studying any other ancient culture. This group, headed by Leopold Zunz (1794–1886), called itself the Society for the Scientific Study of Jewish Culture; its approach is often referred to as the "Science of Judaism" (*Wissenschaft des Judentums*).

Heinrich Graetz, Historian

Among the adherents of Zunz's school was Heinrich Graetz (1817–1891), a man of great talent and imagination. Graetz, a professor at the rabbinical seminary of Breslau, devoted 17 years of his life to the task of writing a well-documented history of the Jews. The first work of its kind, based on solid research and analysis of sources, it is still widely read to this day.

The Struggle for Democracy

As the first half of the 19th century drew to a close, Europe was shaken by uprisings and revolts. When the Revolution of 1848

Printed handkerchief showing an open-air service on the Day of Atonement, 1870, outside Metz.

in Germany was crushed, many of the disappointed freedom fighters left their homeland. Thousands of them crossed the Atlantic to settle in the United States.

The cause of civil liberties in Germany was greatly advanced by the unification in 1871 of all the German lands and provinces into one nation, under the leadership of Prussia. All Germans were recognized as free citizens with equal rights and liberties, including the freedom to worship as they chose. At last the Jews of Germany were free.

A Jewish Wedding by Moritz Oppenheim, 1861. Painting of a German marriage ceremony, showing a tallit serving as a huppah canopy.

Heinrich Graetz, professor and leading modern historian.

The Jews Resettle in England / 1656

Rothschild and Montefiore

Across the Channel from France, England had become a major world power. This land of seafarers and merchants had attracted many Jewish immigrants since the days when Rabbi Manasseh Ben Israel had first come from Holland to plead for the readmission of Jews. Even before his meeting with Oliver Cromwell, individual New Christians had managed to find their way to England. In 1594 one of them, Roderigo Lopez, the personal physician of Queen Elizabeth I, was executed for plotting to poison her.

The first Jews to settle in England in the 17th century were Marranos. They were followed by Sephardic Jews from Italy and Ashkenazim from Germany and Poland. By the 19th century a sizable Jewish community existed in England.

Brothers-in-Law

Among the leading members of Britain's Jewish community was Nathan Mayer Rothschild (1776–1836). His father, Mayer Amschel Rothschild (1743–1812), had built up a major banking business in the German city of Frankfurt. The oldest of Nathan's five brothers had remained in Frankfurt to run the bank there, while the other three had established branches in Paris, Vienna, and Naples. Nathan Rothschild had settled in London, where he became a major figure on the stock exchange and acted as a financial agent for the British government during the Napoleonic Wars.

Moses Montefiore

Another prominent British Jew serving in the war against Napoleon was Nathan Mayer Rothschild's brother-in-law, Moses Montefiore (1784–1885), whose family had come to England from Italy. After his discharge from the British army, Montefiore returned to his business. At the time of the battle of Waterloo, he was a successful stockbroker. Through some of their agents on the continent, Rothschild and Montefiore learned of Napoleon's defeat at Waterloo before this good news reached England.

Rothschild and Montefiore were far-sighted financiers. When the British stock exchange appeared on the verge of collapse during the war, they helped stabilize the market with their financial talents.

New Synagogue, Great Helen Street, London, 1860. It is Sukkot. The man on the left is carrying the Torah. The person next to him is holding a lulav and etrog. On each side of the sanctuary is a prayer for the Royal Family, in English and Hebrew.

Jewish Champions of Liberty

Champions of Civil Liberties

Rothschild and Montefiore were both ardent champions of freedom. When England decided to abolish slavery, they assisted the government with a large loan to make the enforcement of the new law possible.

In 1835, David Salomons was elected sheriff of London, and two years later the same post was occupied by Montefiore. At that time Jews in England still could not receive academic degrees and were barred from most public offices because, with the exception of the post of sheriff of London, they entailed an oath requiring an affirmation of the "true faith of a Christian."

Neither Montefiore nor Rothschild and the other Jewish leaders were satisfied with these conditions. They fought for the elimination of the oath and for the right of Jews to hold public office.

The First Jew Enters Parliament

The son of Nathan Rothschild, Baron Lionel de Rothschild (1808–1879), was elected to Parliament four times in ten years, but resigned each time because the required oath of office was Christian in form. In 1858, the rules were finally changed so that Rothschild could take the oath on a Hebrew Bible as the faith of a Jew. He was the first Jewish member of Britain's House of Commons. Eventually a special oath was devised so that Jews could be sworn in to all public offices and hold professional positions.

When Prime Minister Benjamin Disraeli was negotiating for control of the Suez Canal, it was Lionel de Rothschild who provided him with the funds that made the purchase possible.

Benjamin Disraeli (1804–1881) was himself a symbol of the new position of the Jew in England. Although he had been baptized a Christian at an early age, he was proud to be descended from Spanish Jews who had fled from Spain in 1492. A brilliant statesman and trusted advisor to Queen Victoria, Disraeli also wrote novels and political essays. Many of his books deal with Jewish subjects. During his terms as Prime Minister (1867; 1874–1880) Britain gained control of the Suez Canal and solidified its control of India.

Coat of arms adopted by the Rothschild family in 1817.

Mayer Amschel Rothschild.

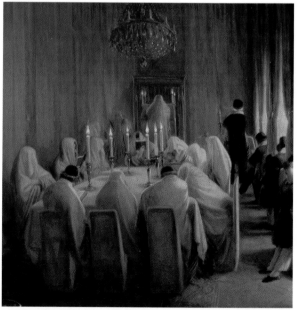

The Rothschild Family at Prayer, by Moritz Daniel Oppenheim.

Moses Montefiore / 1784–1885

Moses Montefiore

In 1838 Moses Montefiore was knighted by Queen Victoria, becoming the first Jew to attain this honor. Although active in public affairs, Sir Moses devoted much of his time and effort to the Board of Deputies of British Jews. As president of that body, he led the Jewish community's effort to secure the removal of the restrictions under which the Jews of England still suffered. One by one, during his long lifetime, the humiliating restrictions were abolished.

The Damascus Libel

In 1840, Sir Moses Montefiore learned that the Jews of Damascus in Syria had been falsely accused of murdering a monk. Jews there were being arrested and tortured, and Jewish children had been imprisoned to compel their parents to confess to a crime they had not committed. Since Syria was under Egyptian jurisdiction, Montefiore, with the backing of the British government, went to Egypt to press for the release of the prisoners and for an official acknowledgment of their innocence. He was accompanied by his wife, Judith, and by a committee he had organized, among whom was Adolphe Crémieux (1796–1880), a French Jew who had fought successfully for the civil rights of the Jews of France.

The incident in Damascus aroused indignation all over the world, and protest demonstrations took place in many countries, including the United States. In the end, the Egyptian government bowed to public pressure. The prisoners were released and their innocence was publicly proclaimed.

Sir Moses and the Tsar

In the vast, isolated land of Russia, the Jews still had no rights. While restrictions were being lifted throughout the rest of Europe, the situation of Russian Jewry was deteriorating. The Jews were still forced to live in the Pale of Settlement and were subjected to humiliating restraints. For centuries they had been artisans, innkeepers, and shopkeepers in the towns and villages of the Pale. Now the tsar wanted them to abandon their customary occupations and relocate to the far-off provinces of Astrakhan and the Caucasus region as farmers.

Moses Montefiore hoped to prevent this cruel decree from being put into effect. In 1846 he and his wife made the long journey to Russia, bearing with them a letter of introduction from Queen Victoria. They made another visit in 1872. Each time they were received courteously at the imperial court. The tsar permitted the Jews to remain in the Pale of Settlement, but nothing was done to alleviate the hardships under which they had to live.

British philanthropist Sir Moses Montefiore. He encouraged many of the early Jewish settlements in Palestine.

Soon after his return home, Montefiore was given the title of baronet by Queen Victoria, who desired to honor him for his courageous efforts on behalf of Jews everywhere.

Sir Moses and Palestine

Realizing that there was little he could do to better the position of his brethren in the lands of the tsar, Montefiore cast about for another solution.

Sir Moses dreamed of the return of the Jews to the Land of Israel. He visited Palestine six times, and each time brought assistance and support to the Jews there, helping them to build hospitals, schools, and synagogues. To attract settlers, he planted vineyards and olive groves, and opened an experimental agricultural school. On the outskirts of the Old City of Jerusalem, Montefiore built a group of homes that became the nucleus of what is now called the New City.

Sir Moses Montefiore lived to the prodigious age of 101. His 100th birthday, in 1884, was marked by elaborate celebrations and parades, for his name had come to be known far and wide as a symbol of charity, progress, and love of liberty.

Windmill in Yemin Moshe, a community named after Moses Montefiore. Much new building has taken place since the time of this photograph and the windmill is still there.

Sir Moses Montefiore speaking to Tsar Nicholas I in 1846 in St. Petersburg.

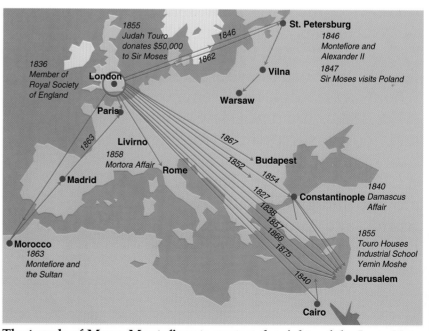

The travels of Moses Montefiore to protect the rights of the Jews. Note the seven trips to the Holy Land.

The Jews of Europe

JEWISH HIGHLIGHTS

The Renaissance 15th–17th century	Jews of Turkey 15th–16th century	Mystics and Kabbalah 15th–16th century	The Netherlands 15th–17th century	Italy 17th century

JEWISH EVENTS • PERSONALITIES • LITERATURE

The Renaissance	Jews of Turkey	Mystics and Kabbalah	The Netherlands	Italy
▷ Shtadlanim	▷ Solomon Ashkenazi	▷ Safed Kabbalah	▷ Amsterdam Dutch Jerusalem	▷ Moses Hayim Luzzatto *The Second Zohar* *The Way of the Righteous*
Joseph Suess Oppenheimer	▷ Doña Gracia Mendes	▷ Rabbi Isaac Luria (Ari) Kabbalah	▷ Marranos	
Yosel of Rosheim	▷ Joseph Nasi Tiberias Silk production	▷ Rabbi Joseph Caro *Shulhan Arukh*	▷ Rabbi Jacob Sasportas	
▷ Ghettos Economic and social restrictions Religious intolerance		▷ False Messiahs David Reubeni Solomon Molcho Shabbatai Zevi	▷ Rabbi Manasseh Ben Israel	
▷ Jewish printers Soncino family			▷ Baruch Spinoza	
▷ Abraham Usque				
▷ Moses de Leon Zohar				
▷ Simeon bar Yohai Lag Ba-Omer				

WORLD HISTORY

The Renaissance	Jews of Turkey	Mystics and Kabbalah	The Netherlands	Italy
▷ Reformation Charles V	▷ Ottoman Empire	▷ Charles V / Spain	▷ Protestant Reformation	▷ Italy
▷ Pope Paul IV Papal Bull	Sultan Suleiman	▷ Constantinople	▷ Dutch colonies	Tiberias
▷ Johann Gutenberg First printed Bible	Selim II		▷ Oliver Cromwell	
▷ Martin Luther	Venice		Rembrandt	
▷ Holy Roman Empire				

The Jews of Europe

JEWISH HIGHLIGHTS

Eastern Europe 16th–18th century	Pale of Settlement 17th–18th century	New Horizons 18th century	Changes in Germany 19th century	English Jews 19th century

JEWISH EVENTS • PERSONALITIES • LITERATURE

Polish Jewry Warsaw Lublin Vilna Posen Cracow	Council of Four Lands abolished	Yiddish	Reform Judaism Rabbi Abraham Geiger	Rothschild Family
Kahal	Council of Lithuania dissolved	Court Jews	Orthodoxy Rabbi Raphael Samson Hirsch	Moses Montefiore Damascus Libel Yemin Moshe
Council of Four Lands	Baal Shem Tov Tzaddikim Hasidim Besht	Moses Mendelssohn German Bible	Historical School Rabbi Zechariah Frankel	Benjamin Disraeli
Yiddish	Gaon of Vilna Mitnagdim	Wilhelm Dohm Edict of Tolerance	Science of Judaism Rabbi Leopold Zunz Heinrich Graetz	
Rabbi Moses Isserles *Shulhan Arukh*				
Cossack Revolt 100,000 Jewish victims				

WORLD HISTORY

King Casimir	Poland loses independence	Frederick the Great	Germany	Suez Canal
King Sigismund	Catherine the Great	Edict of Tolerance Joseph II		Queen Victoria
Cossacks Bogdan Chmielnicki		Napoleon French Revolution (1789) Napoleonic Code Rights of Man		

Looking for Refuge

The expulsion from Spain in 1492 had begun a long period of wandering for many thousands of Jews. Some found new homes in the cities of North Africa, Syria, and the Turkish Empire. Others found further oppression and hardship in other lands; and, all too often, another decree of expulsion.

Those exiles who went to Portugal found themselves betrayed by King Manuel. Thousands were forced to convert to Christianity. Pretending to adopt the new religion in order to save their lives, they remained secret Jews (Marranos), living under the threat of the Inquisition and in constant danger of discovery.

Marranos who were able to leave Portugal often sought refuge in free countries like Holland. Even after generations had passed, some still longed to return to their ancestral religion. Throughout the 16th and 17th centuries, small numbers of devoted secret Jews made their way to Brazil, the West Indies, Mexico, and other New World colonies.

The Colony of Recife

When the Dutch conquered the Portuguese colony of Recife in Brazil in 1630, the Marranos living there joyfully resumed the faith of their ancestors. They were able to join together in public worship and in observing the Sabbath, and openly to teach their children Torah.

To serve as their religious leader and teacher they invited Rabbi Isaac Aboab da Fonseca (1605–1693). Born to Marrano parents in Portugal, Aboab had escaped with his family to Holland and there had studied for the rabbinate. In 1642 he came to Recife from Amsterdam, becoming the first rabbi in the Western Hemisphere.

The freedom of the new Jewish community did not last long. In 1654 the Portuguese reconquered Recife and reintroduced the Inquisition. The Jews, who now were considered heretics, or traitors to the Christian faith, were forced once more to flee for their lives. Isaac Aboab and a few others returned to Amsterdam. Some of the refugees went to the Dutch Caribbean colonies of Surinam and Curaçao.

Isaac Aboab, the first rabbi in the Western Hemisphere. In 1642 he was called to the Dutch Jewish community of Recife, but he returned to Amsterdam when the Portuguese conquered the colony and brought in the Inquisition.

Artist's impression of Recife in the 1600s, the wall of the settlement and the church.

The First Jewish Settlers

First Jews in North America

Twenty-three of the exiles from Recife sailed first to the West Indies, and then, in a vessel named the *Saint Charles*, up the North American coast to the Dutch colony of New Amsterdam. Robbed on the way by pirates, the penniless group arrived in September of 1654 at the port that was later to be named New York.

Peter Stuyvesant

Peter Stuyvesant, the governor appointed by the Dutch West India Company, let the new arrivals know that they were not welcome. He "required them in a friendly way to depart," but allowed them to remain temporarily while he awaited instructions from Amsterdam. After some months, a letter arrived stating that because the Jews of Recife had fought for Holland, and because the Dutch West India Company had many Jewish shareholders, the newcomers were to be permitted to remain, "provided the poor among them shall not become a burden to the company or to the community, but be supported by their own nation."

Burgher Rights

These instructions did not find favor in the eyes of Stuyvesant and his council. Although the company had specified that the Jews were to be treated like everyone else, he denied them the right to stand guard with the colony's other residents, and instead required that they pay a special tax. This policy was abandoned when two Jewish colonists, Jacob Barsimson and Asser Levy, took legal action. Similarly, Abraham de Lucena, Salvador Dandrada, and other Jews filed legal petitions demanding the right to buy homes, to

The Mill Street Synagogue of the *Shearith Israel* Congregation of New York, erected in 1730. This chart for counting the *Omer* between Passover and *Shavuot* was used in the synagogue.

trade, and finally to enjoy full burgher rights.

Three years after they first landed, the Jews of New Amsterdam were granted citizenship. This did not mean that they enjoyed every civil right. They were not permitted to build a synagogue, being required to "exercise in all quietness their religion within their houses." They still had to petition the Dutch Council and later the British governor—for the British conquered the colony and renamed it New York in 1664—when they faced restrictions in trade or professions. Through their outspoken demands for justice and freedom, and their faithfulness to Jewish tradition, this small group of Jews proved themselves worthy ancestors of the American Jewish community.

Asser Levy

In 1657, Asser Levy became the first Jew in New Amsterdam, and therefore in North America, to enjoy the full rights of citizenship. He became the colony's first Jewish landowner when he purchased a plot of land on William Street which is now in the heart of the Wall Street financial district. He was also accorded the privilege of becoming one of its six licensed butchers.

The First Synagogue

In 1664, the British captured New Amsterdam and renamed it New York. Now Asser Levy expanded his business enterprises. In addition he bought a house on Mill Street to be used as a synagogue. Congregation Shearith Israel ("Remnant of Israel"), which had been meeting in private homes, now had its first official building.

Jews in the Colonies

The earliest Jewish settlers in North America were Sephardim, or, as they designated themselves, "of the Portuguese nation." The first synagogue in North America, Shearith Israel in New York, still follows the Spanish and Portuguese minhag, the Sephardic order of prayer. By 1750, however, half of the 300 Jewish residents of New York were Ashkenazim from Central or Eastern Europe.

During the 18th century, small numbers of Jews came to America from Europe, making their homes in Philadelphia, Charleston, Savannah, and other cities along the eastern seaboard.

Rhode Island, the colony founded by Roger Williams as an outpost of religious freedom, was a favorite destination. Among the prominent Jewish residents of Newport, its most important city, was

Interior of the beautiful Newport synagogue, first permanent synagogue in the New World. Named Yeshuat Israel, the congregation and its building were supported for many years by Judah Touro.

Aaron Lopez (1731–1782), son of an old Marrano family in Lisbon, who became a wealthy merchant-shipper in the New World. The Newport synagogue building, one of the earliest to be erected in America, is now a national shrine. It is often called the Touro synagogue in honor of Isaac Touro, its first spiritual leader.

The Chatham Square Cemetery in New York City is one of the oldest Jewish cemeteries in the United States. It was founded in 1656.

The Mill Street Synagogue of the Shearith Israel Congregation of New York, erected in 1730.

The Revolutionary War

There were about 3,000 Jews in the British colonies at the time of the American Revolution. Many of them fought for the patriotic cause. Francis Salvador (1747–1776), a Jewish planter born in England, was chosen a member of the provincial congress in South Carolina in 1774. Two years later, he gave his life in one of the Revolution's first battles.

Among the many other Jewish soldiers was Benjamin Nones (1757–1826), who came from France in order to participate in the battle for freedom and human rights which he felt the Revolution represented. He rose to the rank of major, and afterwards served the new country as a legislator.

Gershom Mendes Seixas

Supporters of the American cause were in danger of imprisonment when the British army occupied New York and Newport. Gershom Mendes Seixas (1745–1816), minister of Shearith Israel, was so outspoken a patriot that he had to flee the city when the British troops landed. Taking the Torah scrolls with him, he reestablished the congregation in Stratford, Connecticut, and then set up a new one, Mikveh Israel, in Philadelphia. In New York after the war, he was honored as a leading religious figure, took part in George Washington's presidential inauguration, and served as a trustee of Columbia College.

Isaac Touro, accompanied by many members of his congregation, fled from Newport when the British occupied it. Aaron Lopez, rather than collaborate with the British, left his wealth and holdings and settled in a small town in Massachusetts until the patriot forces were victorious.

Many volunteers came from across the ocean to join the Americans in their fight for freedom. Among them were Lafayette from France, Pulaski and Kosciusko from Poland, and Baron von Steuben and Baron Johann de Kalb from Germany. The latter, who died in action, commanded a unit of 400 men, so many of whom were Jews that it was sometimes called the Jewish regiment.

Most Canadian colonists remained loyal to England, but a few of them sympathized with the American rebels. David Salisbury Franks (1743–1793), a resident of Montreal, was arrested for making a slighting remark about a statue of King George. After he was released he left Canada and joined the American army.

Haym Salomon

Service beyond the call of duty was rendered by Haym Salomon (1740–1785), a Jewish broker who came to New York from Poland in 1772. Imprisoned for supporting the revolutionary cause, he managed to escape to Philadelphia. There he worked with Robert Morris, superintendent of finance, extending loans and arranging credit to pay for the costs of the war. Though in America only a few years, he was an ardent patriot, never hesitating to risk his own funds to bring about victory for the cause of right.

Aaron Lopez, distinguished citizen of Newport, Rhode Island. He came from a Marrano family in Portugal in 1752.

Washington and the Jews

Words of George Washington

When the new nation came into being, and George Washington became its first President, the Jews of Newport were one of the many groups to send a message of good wishes. They expressed their appreciation for "a Government which to bigotry gives no sanction, to persecution no assistance," and their thanks to God for "all the blessings of civil and religious liberty."

In answer, President Washington stated, "The citizens of the United States of America have a right to applaud themselves for having given to mankind examples of an enlarged and liberal policy. All possess alike liberty of conscience and immunities of citizenship." He continued with a clear statement of the position of the new nation on human liberty:

"It is now no more that toleration is spoken of, as if it was by the indulgence of one class of people, that another enjoyed the exercise of their inherent natural rights. For happily the Government of the United States, which gives to bigotry no sanction, to persecution no assistance, requires only that they who live under its protection should demean themselves as good Citizens, in giving it on all occasions their effectual support."

Freedom of Religion

The United States was the first country in the world to guarantee full freedom of religion. The First Amendment to the Constitution begins: "Congress shall make no law respecting the establishment of religion, or prohibiting the free exercise thereof." Although some states still had laws restricting the right of holding office to those of recognized Christian faith, all of these were soon challenged and revoked. Jews were able to take their place as active citizens of the new democracy.

Chicago's memorial to Haym Salomon, seen standing to the right of George Washington while Robert Morris stands on his left, both supporting him in his fight for freedom.

This painting by Ferris shows the forging of the Liberty Bell. It was cast by the Whitechapel Bell Foundry in England and cost £100. The inscription on the bell is from Leviticus, the third book of the Bible. It reads "Proclaim liberty throughout the land, to all its inhabitants." The Liberty Bell is now in Philadelphia

Tombstone of Private Moses Judah, a soldier in the Revolutionary War. He served in the Pennsylvania Militia.

Men of Prominence

Ezra Stiles, a christian, was president of Yale College from 1778 to 1795, found much to praise in the Jewish citizens. Speaking of Aaron Lopez, he said, "His beneficence to his family, to his nation, and to all the world is without a parallel." Other Jews in early America also displayed the philanthropy and the desire to serve others that characterize the American Jewish community to this day.

Judah Touro, philanthropist of New Orleans, in his old age.

Mordecai Manuel Noah (1785–1851), writer, politician, and well-known public figure.

Judah Touro

One of the many civic-minded Jews was the wealthy New Orleans merchant Judah Touro (1775–1854), who willed his entire fortune to synagogues, schools, hospitals, and orphan homes in 18 cities. A patriotic soldier who was seriously wounded in the battle of New Orleans during the War of 1812, Touro gave the largest contribution, $10,000, for the building of the Bunker Hill Monument. A large portion of his estate went to build homes for the poor in Jerusalem, under the direction of Sir Moses Montefiore.

Mordecai Manuel Noah

A quite different public figure was Mordecai Manuel Noah (1785–1851), well known as a politician, playwright, and newspaper editor. For a short time he was American consul at Tunis, there learning about the poverty and persecution suffered by the Jews of North Africa. In a grand gesture, Noah rallied support and proclaimed the establishment of Ararat, a settlement on Grand Island in New York's Niagara River, as a "city of refuge" for the oppressed Jews of the world. Until the ancient homeland in Palestine was restored, he declared, the United States, as the world's premier free nation, would be the proper host for the persecuted of Israel.

Ezra Stiles, president of Yale.

The Jewish Commodore

The spirit of adventure and a sense of justice motivated Uriah Phillips Levy (1792–1862) throughout his life. At the age of 10 he ran off and enlisted as a cabin boy on a sailing ship. By 20 he had become a master seaman and was given the command of a U.S. warship, the *George Washington.* The sailors resented taking orders from so young a young commander and mutinied. They marooned him on a deserted island from which he was rescued by a British ship. When he refused to enlist in the British navy, he was put in irons, but at the first port he managed to escape.

Adventure and Bravado

When the United States and Britain went to war in 1812, Levy was assigned to the warship *Argus.* It sank or captured more than 20 British cargo vessels. Levy was put in command of one of the captured ships and ordered to sail it to Philadelphia. Once again, the spirit of adventure and bravado got the better of him. On the way he audaciously attacked a heavily-armed British warship. His ship was sunk and Levy once again became a British prisoner.

The Duel

After sitting out the rest of the war in an English prison, Levy was repatriated and commissioned a lieutenant in the U.S. Navy. When several of his fellow officers baited him by making anti-Semitic remarks, Levy refused to back down. He challenged one of them to a duel and killed him. Since dueling had been outlawed, Levy was court-martialed and dismissed from the navy, but later he was exonerated by a board of inquiry and returned to service. During the course of his career he was court-martialed five more times on various charges, but was always cleared.

Levy Challenges Naval Justice

Levy next challenged the use of corporal punishment aboard naval vessels. Sailors on U.S. ships were regularly flogged and starved even for minor infractions. Levy refused to use corporal punishment on ships he commanded. He went on to persuade Congress that something had to be done to stop this sadistic practice. In 1850, thanks to Levy's heroic efforts, Congress abolished corporal punishment in the navy.

Uriah Phillips Levy (1792–1862)
Fighting sailor and admirer of Thomas Jefferson. He helped abolish corporal punishment in the U. S. Navy.

Many ranking naval officers resented what Levy had done. In retaliation they had him court-martialed on trumped-up charges.

Once again Levy challenged the sentence. Acting as his own counsel, he put on a defense so impressive that the judges did not even leave the room to vote. He was acquitted and returned to active duty with the rank of captain. Two years later he was promoted to commodore, the highest rank in the U.S. Navy at that time.

Respect and Honor

Despite the insults and hardships, Uriah P. Levy loved America. A great admirer of Thomas Jefferson, he purchased his home at Monticello and restored it as a historical shrine. In 1943 the navy honored his memory by naming a new destroyer the U.S.S. *Levy.* In 1959 the Jewish chapel at the naval base in Norfolk, Virginia, was named the Commodore Levy Chapel.

Immigration and Westward Expansion

Encouraged by the promise of liberty and opportunity, great numbers of Europeans migrated to America during the 19th century. The Industrial Revolution was changing the way of life in the Old World, and many displaced workers and farmers sought new homes in the New World. The era of political reaction following the Napoleonic Wars and the failure of the revolutions of the 1840s in Central Europe led those who longed for freedom to turn their eyes across the Atlantic Ocean.

The Hand of Freedom

Millions of people in Europe saw the New World as the promised land of freedom. There had been revolutions in France and other countries, but the reactionary governments that gained power after Napoleon's defeat at Waterloo had no sympathy for the ideals of the French Revolution. They reinstated many of the old restrictive laws, and as a result, full equality and civil rights again became dreams.

As always, life was most difficult for Jews. Even in the 1820s and 1830s, but especially after the failed uprisings of 1848, Jews from Central Europe and the German states began flocking to America. At the time of the Revolution, there were about 3,000 Jews in the United States. By 1840 there were 40,000, the majority of them immigrants or the children of immigrants.

The newcomers became part of a growing country with open borders. When they arrived in America, they found well-established communities of fellow Jews in New York, Philadelphia, Baltimore, Richmond, Charleston, New Orleans, and many other cities. As early as the 1790s adventurous Jews had traveled alone into the interior to set up trading posts or start new farms in such areas as Natchez, Mississippi, and Montgomery, Alabama. John Law, a Jew from Montreal, was trading with Indians at Green Bay, Wisconsin, around the year 1800, and Samuel Solomon came to St. Louis in 1805.

The German Jews

Many of the new German immigrants, both Jewish and non-Jewish, settled in the Midwestern cities of Cleveland, Cincinnati, Milwaukee, and Detroit. All through the Midwest one could hear German spoken in the small Jewish communities. Synagogues were started in Cincinnati in 1824 and in Chicago in 1847.

Jewish immigrants worked at many different kinds of jobs. Their number included laborers, farmers, ranchers, watchmakers, tailors, doctors, lawyers, printers and editors, boatmen, and wagon drivers. A very substantial proportion were peddlers and storekeepers.

Julius Meyer (1851–1909) of Omaha. Nebraska, an Indian trader in the 1870s, with some of his Indian friends. Meyer spoke several Indian dialects.

Jewish Peddlers

Many of the Jewish immigrants who came to these shores became peddlers. With settlements spreading far and wide across the country, there was a need for men to travel from place to place, bring, needed goods to people on farms and in villages too small to support a store. Some peddlers plied their routes through the countryside on foot, carrying their goods in backpacks; others drove small wagons. The wares they offered ranged from needles and pins, combs and mirrors, ribbons and cloth, to pots and pans, knives, and books. Depending on the circumstances and the area they worked in, some returned home every weekend, others only every few weeks or months.

Though they usually received a warm welcome from their customers, especially because they were important sources of news, the Jewish peddlers led a hard life. Travel was difficult and dangerous. They were lonely and homesick. They might go many weeks without meeting a fellow Jew or another person who could speak their native language.

afternoon, "unwashed, unshaven, in a gentile inn," far from home and friends.

The peddlers were ambitious and hard-working. Many of them went on to open stores in new settlements, especially places located near roads or river landings. They saved their money and, as soon as possible, sent for their wives, parents, and siblings in the old country.

Once a few Jewish families had settled in the same area, a Jewish community would come into existence. Almost always it began by purchasing a cemetery and holding weekly prayer services. Before long a shohet would be hired to provide kosher meat, and a teacher engaged for the children. Larger groups would try to bring a rabbi or hazzan. With this done, the former peddlers came to feel at home in the new country.

Some Jewish storekeepers went on to become department store magnates. Among the many major stores founded or expanded by Jews were Filene's in Boston, Macy's in New York, Rich's in Atlanta, and Magnin's in San Francisco.

The Jewish Religion

One of the hardest things was not being able to keep kosher and to observe the Sabbath and other holidays. A letter written by one peddler says that he was about to start the Sabbath on Friday

Evening Service
Simeon OF *Levy*
ROSHASHANAH,
AND
KIPPUR,
OR
The BEGINNING of the YEAR,
AND
The DAY of ATONEMENT.

NEW-YORK:
Printed by *W. Weyman*, in *Broad-Street*, MDCCLXI.

The first High Holiday prayer book published in America.

Macy's, one of the world's largest department stores, was founded by Lazarus Straus in partnership with R. H. Macy. Straus moved to New York City from Atlanta because of the Civil War.

Women of Valor

Rebecca Gratz

Jewish women in this country were active in the fields of education and good deeds. Lovely Rebecca Gratz (1781–1869), of a distinguished Philadelphia family, founded the first Jewish Sunday School in America, and worked for orphanages and other welfare institutions. It is thought that she was the inspiration for the virtuous heroine who bears her name in Sir Walter Scott's *Ivanhoe.*

Penina Moïse

Penina Moïse (1797–1880), an educator and writer, supervised the Jewish Sunday School in Charleston, South Carolina, and composed poems and hymns throughout her life, even though she became blind in middle age.

Penina Moïse was for many years the poet laureate of Charleston. She was born in 1797 to French-speaking parents who had escaped from a slave rebellion in the West Indies.

Young Penina studied by herself and was familiar with the Bible along with the writings of Homer and Shakespeare and authors of her own day. For many years she was the superintendent of the Sunday School of Congregation Beth Elohim in Charleston. Though she wrote poetry for newspapers and magazines, her favorite was writing hymns based on the psalms.

Penina and her brother Abraham were active in the group of members of Beth Elohim that wanted to modernize the service along lines similar to those advocated by the reformers in Germany. Among other things, they wanted to have choral singing and organ music to make the services attractive, and sermons in English to explain the Torah readings.

In 1841, Beth Elohim dedicated its new building. A hymn written by Penina Moïse was used at the service. Her long life was one of reading, writing, and teaching, activities which she continued, as much as possible, during her last 25 years, when she was blind and bedridden.

Emma Lazarus

The outstanding Jewish writer of this period was Emma Lazarus (1849–1887), whose early poetry on themes of nature and mythology won the praise of Ralph Waldo Emerson. The persecution of the Jews of Russia, and the steady stream of immigrants from Eastern Europe, made the young woman more aware of her people and faith. She studied Hebrew and Jewish history, gaining new pride and loyalty and a powerful theme for her later writings.

Songs of a Semite and *By the Waters of Babylon* are collections of poems by Lazarus expressing sympathy for her people's past and hope for the future. "Let but an Ezra rise anew," she wrote, "to lift the banner of the Jew!" Her best-known poem is "The New Colossus," inscribed on a plaque in the base of the Statue of Liberty in New York harbor.

Portrait of Rebecca Gratz by Thomas Sully.

Title page of a book by Penina Moïse.

California, Here We Come!

In the year 1848 gold was discovered in California. Word spread swiftly across the country. "Gold, gold!" California was on everyone's tongue.

The Forty-niners

The Gold Rush began in 1849. There were many Jews among the Forty-niners, as those who joined the rush were called. Some hoped to find gold, others planned on becoming land developers, merchants, or professionals in the new towns springing up in California.

In the very first year of the Gold Rush, there were enough Jews in San Francisco to hold High Holiday services. Over the next few years, Jewish congregations were founded in many of the state's smaller towns.

Levi Strauss

Levi Strauss (1829–1902) was a German-born immigrant who arrived in New York in 1848. Two years later he caught the "gold fever" and sailed for San Francisco by way of Cape Horn, at the tip of South America. He arrived in California with a pack of needles, pins, string, sewing thread, and bolts of cloth. In no time, Strauss sold all of his stock except a few bolts of heavy canvas. He tried to sell the canvas to a miner for a tent, but the man said he needed a strong pair of pants much more. Strauss made all his canvas into pants. When these sold out, he ordered special denim cloth from France and dyed it blue.

Levi Strauss's name appeared on a red tag on every pair of pants he manufactured, and before long a new term for those pants was added to the English language: Levi's. Today, the Levi Strauss Co. is a multinational enterprise with factories in

Advertisement for denim work clothes produced by Levi Strauss & Co.

many countries. Strauss's descendants are active in Jewish affairs and have contributed to the support of Jewish institutions all over the world.

Pioneers and Civic Leaders

From the start, Jews helped to build up the new state of California. Some became fur traders, miners, grape growers, or cattle dealers. Adolf Sutro (1830–1898), the German-born engineer who built the great mine tunnel that carries his name in Nevada, served as mayor of San Francisco from 1895 to 1897.

Solomon Heydenfeldt and Henry A. Lyons were elected to the California Supreme Court. Other Jews were civic leaders in Los Angeles and other cities.

One Jew, Solomon Nunes Carvalho (1815–1897), a painter and photographer, accompanied the great explorer John C. Fremont on an expedition to map the land route to California in 1853. With him, he crossed the desert and climbed the Rocky Mountains, almost losing his life on the way. When Carvalho arrived in the city of Los Angeles, he sought out the local Jews and helped establish the Hebrew Benevolent Society there.

Workers in the Sutro tunnel.

Jews, the Civil War, the Union

The Civil War found most American Jews remaining loyal to the section of the country in which they lived. Jews were officers and fighting men on both sides.

In the years of controversy before the war, many Jews were active in the anti-slavery movement. Kansas Jews joined John Brown's army in the fight against slavery. Journalists like Moritz Pinner wrote articles in favor of abolition.

Moritz Pinner for the Union

Moritz edited the *Kansas Post,* a newspaper that tried to make Kansas a free state. This was a dangerous period, because there was a gang called "Border Ruffians," made up of people who wanted Kansas to be a slave state. They attacked those who opposed slavery.

Pinner was a delegate to the Republican Convention in 1860 which nominated Abraham Lincoln for the presidency. He later refused a government post that would have taken him to Honduras; he wanted to stay and fight for the Union.

Rabbis for the Union

Two outspoken rabbis, Sabato Morais (1832–1897) of Philadelphia and David Einhorn (1809–1879) of Baltimore, boldly preached against slavery despite strong opposition in their respective cities. The hostility against them was so intense that on one occasion, during the secession riots of 1861, Rabbi Einhorn had to flee Baltimore.

Soldiers for the Union

The surgeon general of the North was Jonathan Phineas Horowitz. The many Jewish officers in the Union army included several brigadier generals. One of them was Philip Joachimsen, who had helped to convict slave traders while serving as a U.S. attorney in New York.

Jewish Heroes

Edward Solomon, another general, led an Illinois regiment in which there were over 100 Jews. After the war he became governor of the Washington Territory. There were more than 6,000 Jewish soldiers in the Union army, many of them serving in units that were predominantly Jewish. From Pennsylvania came Cameron's Dragoons, commanded by Col. Max Friedman. Many Jewish soldiers died on the battlefield or in Confederate prison camps. Seven Congressional Medals of Honor were awarded to Jews in the Union army.

Michael M. Allen, of Philadelphia, served as unofficial chaplain of Cameron's Dragoons, a Pennsylvania cavalry regiment. The regiment was commanded by Col. Max Friedman.

August Bondi (1833–1907), abolitionist. After leaving Austria following the Revolution of 1848 , he, with Jacob Benjamin and Theodore Weiner, joined John Brown's anti-slavery army in Kansas.

Jews, the Civil War, the Confederacy

The Confederate Army

There were also thousands of Jewish soldiers on the Confederate side. The South's Secretary of War declared at one point that he could not give furloughs to Jewish soldiers for the High Holidays since there were at least 10,000 of them—more than could be spared from their posts.

The most important Jew serving the Confederacy was Judah Philip Benjamin of Louisiana (1811–1884). Elected to the U.S. Senate in 1852, Benjamin left Washington when Louisiana seceded from

Judah P. Benjamin (1811–1884), Confederate Secretary of War and Secretary of State. After the war he fled to England.

the Union. At various times he served as the Confederacy's Attorney General, Secretary of War, and Secretary of State.

Although he did not regard himself as a Jew, Benjamin was called an Israelite by his enemies on both sides of the conflict. A northerner described him as an "Israelite with Egyptian principles."

When the South began to lose the war, Benjamin's political enemies in the Confederacy placed the blame on his shoulders. After the war he escaped to England and became an attorney.

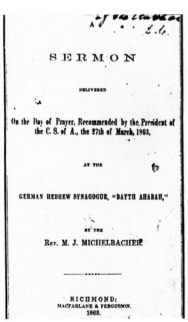

The President of the Confederate States of America, Jefferson Davis, on March 27, 1863, recommended a Day of Prayer. Rev. Michelbacher, of the German synagogue in Richmond, preached this sermon, to which he added a prayer for the Confederacy.

Captain Asher W. Garber.

Private Thomas Jefferson Goldman.

List of Confederate Jewish soldiers buried by Rev. George Jacobs.

General Robert E. Lee's battle-tested Army of Northern Virginia included many Jewish soldiers. Captain Asher W. Garber was an officer in the Virginia Light Artillery and Private Thomas Jefferson Goldman served in the 44th Georgia Infantry.

Isaac Leeser / 1806–1868

Isaac Leeser (1806–1868), the most activist American rabbi of his day, set about almost single-handed to try to remedy all the lacks in Jewish life and education. He published textbooks, and translations of the Bible and the prayerbook. In his Philadelphia congregation, Mikveh Israel, he delivered vigorous sermons in English, advocating intensified education and Jewish unity. In 1867, with the help of Sabato Morais, he established Maimonides College, an institution for formal Jewish studies, but it had few financial supporters and soon closed its doors.

Isaac Leeser (1806–1868), rabbi, teacher, translator, and organizer, did much to further Jewish education and raise the standard of Jewish communal life.

Isaac Leeser traveled to Albany, New York, to discuss American Jewry's problems and needs with Rabbi Isaac Mayer Wise. For many years afterwards, there were discussions between Wise and Leeser, both in person and in print. The two had different ideas about how to be a good Jew, but both wanted to unify American's Jews, and to strengthen their faith and knowledge.

It was not very difficult to bring Jews together when there was a crisis. Ten years after the Damascus libel of 1840, for instance, the United States and Switzerland were negotiating a treaty intended to open up each country to the citizens of the other for travel and business. The Swiss made it plain that American Jews would not be permitted in those parts of Switzerland that banned Jewish residents. If the United States accepted this, it would mean that it was not treating its Jewish citizens as worthy of the full protection of their government.

American Jewry protested vociferously, and so did many non-Jews, among them such distinguished political figures as Daniel Webster and Henry Clay.

The "Occident"

Isaac Leeser made his greatest contribution as editor of the *Occident*, a magazine that appeared monthly from 1843 to 1869. Its pages tell of the interests and problems of American Jews in those years, including items ranging from the arrival of a new Hebrew teacher in New York to protests against the kidnapping of an Italian Jewish boy, Edgar Mortara, by the Catholic church in 1858. At times of crisis, magazines like the *Occident*, David Einhorn's *Sinai,* and Isaac Mayer Wise's *Israelite* served to inform and in some measure to unite the Jews of America.

THE OCCIDENT,

AND

AMERICAN JEWISH ADVOCATE.

A MONTHLY PERIODICAL

DEVOTED TO

THE DIFFUSION OF KNOWLEDGE

ON

Jewish Literature and Religion.

EDITED

BY ISAAC LEESER.

ללמוד וללמד לשמור ולעשות
" To learn and to teach, to observe and to do."

For 25 years, Isaac Leeser edited and published the *Occident*, a leading Jewish periodical, which gave its readers essays, stories, poems, and news of Jewish communities all over the world.

Early Attempts at Reform

The free atmosphere and lack of central authority in pioneer America encouraged religious reform and innovation. In 1824, a group called the Reformed Society of Israelites broke away from Congregation Beth Elohim in Charleston. Led by Isaac Harby (1788–1828), a young writer, the Society issued its own prayerbook and for several years conducted services in English.

The Reform movement in the United States became stronger in the 1840s with the arrival of large numbers of Jews from Germany, including several rabbis who agreed with the ideas expressed by Abraham Geiger. While upholding the ethics and moral law of Judaism, they wished to adapt to modern times by abolishing rituals and ideals which they felt no longer had meaning.

Rabbi David Einhorn (1809–1879) came to Baltimore and Rabbi Samuel Hirsch (1815–1889) to Philadelphia with radical ideas. They no longer considered Judaism's ritual laws to be binding. They felt that the age-old hopes for the coming of the Messiah and the return to Zion had no meaning for American Jews. They dropped many Hebrew prayers, substituting German readings and hymns.

Other Reform rabbis, who had more moderate views and wished to preserve some of Judaism's ancient traditions, were Bernhard Felsenthal of Chicago (1822–1908) and Max Lilienthal of Cincinnati (1815–1882).

The Torah Ark of Congregation Beth Elohim, Charleston, South Carolina, is a replica of the one destroyed by fire in 1838. The original Ark was built in 1799.

Rabbi David Einhorn (1809–1879), radical Reform leader and outspoken abolitionist, served pulpits in Philadelphia and New York after leaving Baltimore at the time of pro-slavery riots.

MISCELLANEOUS WRITINGS

OF THE LATE

ISAAC HARBY, ESQ.

ARRANGED AND PUBLISHED BY HENRY L. PINCKNEY AND ABRAHAM MOISE, FOR THE BENEFIT OF HIS FAMILY.

TO WHICH IS PREFIXED,

A MEMOIR OF HIS LIFE,

BY ABRAHAM MOISE.

Charleston:
PRINTED BY JAMES S. BURGES,
NO. 44 QUEEN-STREET.
1829.

Title page of a collection of writings by Isaac Harby, published after his death by his associate in community and religious endeavors, Abraham Moïse.

Isaac Mayer Wise / 1819–1900

Father of Reform

The leading organizer of Reform Judaism in America was Isaac Mayer Wise (1819–1900). As rabbi of congregations in Albany, New York, and then in Cincinnati, he introduced English readings and sermons, instrumental music, Confirmation for both boys and girls, and the one-day observance of holidays instead of two. He founded and for years edited the weekly *Israelite*, advocating in its pages that American Jewry unite. He compiled a prayerbook, hoping to establish a minhag America, a uniform mode of observance and worship in which both traditional and Reform Jews could join.

Hebrew Union College

Calling together congregational leaders from 28 cities, Rabbi Wise, in 1873, founded the Union of American Hebrew Congregations. The next year he established and became the head of the Hebrew Union College in Cincinnati, America's first institution for higher Jewish education and the training of rabbis.

Wise was not able to induce American Jewry to adopt one pattern of belief and worship. The radical reformers of the eastern cities believed that he was unwilling to go far enough; they did not agree with his devotion to the

Rabbi Isaac Mayer Wise

use of Hebrew in the service and his insistence that the Sabbath be observed on Saturday instead of being transferred to the commonly accepted American day of rest, Sunday.

On the other hand, Orthodox or traditional Jews could not accept Wise's reforms in the service, his abolition of many rituals,

and his denial of basic ideals like the return to Zion.

American Jewry, though it did not unite under his leadership, learned from Rabbi Wise how to organize and strengthen its religious life.

Title page of the first Reform prayerbook to appear in America. Prepared by a commission consisting of Rabbis Kalish, Wise, and Rothenheim, it was issued in English, German, and Hebrew.

Very early photograph of the Hebrew Union College building in Cincinnati, Ohio.

The American Experience Begins

JEWISH HIGHLIGHTS

| Jewish Refugees 17th century | First American Jews 17th century | Revolutionary War 18th Century | Men and Women of Prominence (18th–19th century) | Immigration 19th century | American Reform Movement 19th century |

JEWISH EVENTS • PERSONALITIES • LITERATURE

Jewish Refugees	First American Jews	Revolutionary War	Men and Women of Prominence	Immigration	American Reform Movement
▶ Recife Rabbi Isaac Aboab	▶ New Amsterdam Asser Levy First synagogue Aaron Lopez ▶ Shearith Israel Sephardim	▶ Francis Salvador ▶ Benjamin Nones ▶ Mikveh Israel Gershom Mendes Seixas ▶ Isaac Touro ▶ Haym Salomon ▶ David Salisbury Franks	Judah Touro Mordecai Manuel Noah Ezra Stiles Uriah Phillips Levy Levi Strauss Rebecca Graetz Emma Lazarus Penina Moïse	German Jews Peddlers ▶ Jewish peddlers– Department stores Filene's ▶ R. H. Macy's Lazarus Straus Magnin's ▶ Rich's ▶ CIVIL WAR Moritz Pinner August Bondi ▶ Rabbi Sabato Morais ▶ Rabbi David Einhorn ▶ Edward Solomon ▶ August Bondi ▶ Michael M. Allen ▶ Judah Benjamin	Rabbi Isaac Leeser The *Occident* Rabbi David Einhorn Rabbi Isaac Mayer Wise Union of American Hebrew Congregations Reform Prayerbook Isaac Harby

WORLD HISTORY

▶ Recife ▶ Surinam ▶ Curaçao	▶ Holland Peter Stuyvesant ▶ Rhode Island Roger Williams	▶ George Washington Baron von Steuben Marquis de Lafayette ▶ Liberty Bell	▶ California	▶ Poland ▶ Russia	

Tsar Nicholas I and the Jews

Not even the intervention of so prominent a person as Sir Moses Montefiore could bring about an improvement in the situation of Russian Jewry. Tsar Nicholas I, who came to the throne of Russia in 1825, was bent on assimilating the diverse population of his empire into one vast Russian nation. During the reign of his brother, Alexander I (1777–1825), Napoleon's army had marched east, deep into the very heart of Russia. Russia had defended itself well and the French armies had retreated. But the new ideas of freedom and equality that had arisen in France had been carried by its soldiers into the lands of the tsar. Poland, which never had accepted Russia's rule gracefully, now chafed under its reins.

Tsar Alexander II (1818–1881)

Oath of a Jewish recruit from Stolin, sworn in the synagogue of Pinsk, 1829. This Jewish youth, under the 1827 statute of Tsar Nicholas I, was forced to serve in the Russian army. The document is printed in Hebrew with handwritten additions in Russian.

Governmental Pressures

To gain greater control over the minorities in his realm, Nicholas I instituted a double administrative policy. On the one hand he lifted some of the restrictions that had been imposed upon them, but at the same time he sought to divest them of their identities as separate nationality groups. He dealt a severe blow to the Jews of the Pale of Settlement when he ordered the Kahal, the time-honored instrument of Jewish communal self-government, to disband.

The tsar wanted the Jews to give up their Yiddish language, their religion, and their traditions. He also wanted a large and powerful army, and to realize this aim he instituted a draft of young men at the age of 18, for a term of 25 years. Jews, however, were drafted at the age of 12 and had to serve for 31 years. Recruiters would come and take Jewish boys from their homes by force. Once they were in the army, they would be pressured to convert. Frequently they would be beaten and starved in an effort to persuade them to renounce their faith.

Crown Schools

As another means of hastening the disappearance of Russian Jewry as a distinct group, Tsar Nicholas I set up special schools in the Pale of Settlement. In these crown schools, as they were called, Jewish children were to learn Russian and be given an education that would wean them away from their traditional way of life and toward conversion to Christianity.

Despite the pressures brought upon them by the tsarist government, the Jews of Russia remained loyal to their heritage. The community was hard-pressed. Many were forced to leave the villages of the Pale and move to cities where they had no way to earn a living. When the tsar realized that his Jewish policy was not bringing about conversions, he invoked sterner restrictions.

Alexander II, a Liberal Ruler

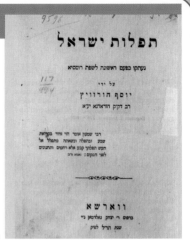

Nicholas I died in 1855 and was succeeded by his son, Alexander II, a man of liberal leanings. In 1861, Alexander abolished serfdom, making it possible for peasants to buy land and establish farms. The Jews of the Pale of Settlement hoped that soon their lot, too, would be improved.

Their hopes were realized in great measure, for Alexander II abolished the draft of Jewish boys.

Alexander wanted to keep pace with developments in Western Europe by furthering the growth of Russia's factories and industrial centers. He permitted Jews to move from the Pale to the large cities and encouraged them to go into manufacturing, learn trades, become merchants, and take professional training at the universities.

Many educated Jews believed that a secular education was compatible with Jewish culture. Judah Leib Gordon (1831–1892), an important poet and journalist, coined the motto "Be a man outside, but a Jew in your own home."

No longer did all Jews have to live in the Pale of Settlement. Some became respected and successful merchants and manufacturers; others practiced law and medicine in the large cities. Still others became skilled workers in the new industrial centers.

Alexander II Assassinated

Russia was a hotbed of revolutionary movements. Despite the reforms, many Jewish youngsters joined the revolutionary parties. In 1881 Tsar Alexander II was assassinated. The assailant was caught and implicated his fellow plotters, one of whom was a Jewish girl named Gessia Helfman. Government officials used this incident to incite pogroms against the

Title page of the first prayer book Tifilot Yisrael *ever translated into Russian. The* siddur *was translated by Rabbi Joseph Hurwitz in 1869. It was published in Warsaw, the capital of the Polish provinces of the Russian Empire.*

Jews. Over the next two years thousands of Jews were murdered, and innumerable businesses and homes looted and destroyed. To make matters worse, the reforms instituted by Alexander were rescinded by his successor, and the government issued the May Laws, which restricted Jewish residence and professional rights.

The pogroms of 1881–82 in Russia and Ukraine were decisive in establishing Zionism as a major movement. The outbreak of violence on such a broad scale, and with government collusion, made many Jews feel that they could never lead a normal life in Russia. While some decided to emigrate to the United States, others concluded that the only viable solution was Eretz Yisrael, the Land of Israel.

After the Pogrom by Maurice Minkowski (1881–1930). The pogroms claimed thousands of Jewish victims.

The Haskalah

The Haskalah ("Enlightenment") was a movement in Judaism that introduced modern ideas and religious approaches and advocated mastery of secular knowledge. Its adherents often pursued secular professions and abandoned practices that differentiated them from their non-Jewish neighbors—wearing modern clothing, trimming their beards, and speaking Russian or German instead of Yiddish. Although opposed by many Orthodox rabbis and by Hasidim, the Haskalah made rapid progress, initially in Germany and Western Europe, and later in Russia, especially among members of the Jewish middle class.

The new ideas of enlightenment that first arose in the West found their way into the Pale of Settlement as early as the reign of Nicholas I, arousing interest in secular learning. This trend was furthered by the newly-established crown schools, which taught history, Russian, and science in addition to religious subjects.

Hebrew Reborn

In Western Europe, the Haskalah had lured many Jews away from their heritage—but not so in the East. There it took the direction, not of assimilation, but of a more intense cultivation of the Hebrew language and modern Hebrew literature along with secular knowledge. Thus began the rebirth of Hebrew as a living language. Hebrew and Yiddish writers applied their talents to immortalize the folkways and customs of the Jews of the Pale, their ideals and their daily lives. In their works, both prose and poetry, they described the negative as well as the positive aspects of life in Russia, thereby stimulating their readers to social and intellectual development.

Judah Leib Gordon

Among the great exponents of Russian Haskalah were several authors whose works left an indelible mark in the annals of modern Hebrew literature and culture: Abraham Mapu (1808–1867), pioneer Hebrew novelist famed for *Ahavat Zion,* a biblical romance written in a classical Hebrew style; Judah Leib Gordon (1831–1892), greatest of the 19th-century Hebrew poets, who fought valiantly against what he considered primitive customs, but remained loyal to Jewish tradition; and Yitzhak Ber Levinsohn (1788–1860), erudite author of works demonstrating the complete harmony of Torah and the scientific spirit.

Yitzhak Ber Levinsohn

The Development of Yiddish Literature

Mendele Mokher Sefarim

Many authors wrote in Yiddish, the everyday language of the Jewish people of Russia and Poland. One of the best-loved Yiddish writers was Sholem Yaakov Abramovich (1836–1917), who used the pen-name Mendele Mokher Seforim ("Mendele the Bookseller"). He started his career as a Hebrew author, and, in fact, is also counted as one of the founders of modern Hebrew prose. It is, however, as a Yiddish writer that he gained special fame. He painted a vivid picture of life in the towns of the Pale, and his books were read

Sholem Aleichem and family.

with great enthusiasm. The writings of Mendele and others revealed Yiddish for the first time as an expressive language, capable of reflecting the thought and character of the Jews of Eastern Europe.

Sholem Aleichem

Among the other great luminaries of Yiddish literature was Sholem Aleichem (pen-name of Shalom Rabinowitz, 1859–1916). He created the character of Tevye der Milchiger ("Tevye the Milkman"), a lighthearted pauper who drives his rickety wagon in search of a living, but whose thoughts reach up to God. The story of Tevye has been retold as *Fiddler on the Roof,* one of the most successful

musicals ever performed. *Fiddler on the Roof* has been staged in many languages and its message has universal appeal.

Sholem Aleichem went to the United States for the first time in 1906 and again upon the outbreak of World War I. The sketches he wrote in his last years give insight into the immigrant generation on American soil.

Isaac Leib Peretz

Isaac Leib Peretz (1852–1915) was one of the founders and giants of modern Yiddish literature. He was a prosperous lawyer, but because of governmental restrictions was forced to find another job. Eventually, Peretz was placed in charge of the Jewish cemeteries. This position was a blessing in disguise, since it provided him with the opportunity to concentrate on writing stories, plays, and poems both in Yiddish and in Hebrew.

With simplicity and power, Peretz's prolific pen produced a stream of stories about the common people. He felt for their misery, and discovered in their lives the virtues of love, faith, and heroism. His Hasidic stories reflect his religious background and position the Rebbe as the ideal for the messianic future.

Mendele Mokher Seforim

Persecutions and Pogroms

Arrests and Accusations

Alexander II was succeeded by his son Alexander III. Determined to establish his rule securely at all costs, the new tsar was coldly indifferent to the well-being of his people.

Like the rulers of the Middle Ages, he looked for a defenseless minority group that could be blamed for the country's troubles. Naturally, the choice fell on the Jews. Alexander accused them of fomenting revolt and of having been involved in the assassination of his father. He persecuted anyone suspected of inciting rebellion. Many were arrested and shot; others were sentenced to long prison terms in the freezing wastelands of Siberia.

Pogroms Spur Emigration

The tsar had a special punishment in store for his chosen scapegoat. Government officials and agents stirred up the Russian people with anti-Semitic speeches, inciting them to attack the Jewish community. Jews were brutally beaten and many lost their lives.

The years 1881–82 were marked by terrible pogroms that shocked and saddened Jews the world over. In two years, thousands of Jews were murdered. Innumerable Jewish businesses and homes were looted and destroyed.

Anti-Jewish legislative measures accompanied the pogroms. Alexander II's reforms were rescinded. The May Laws in 1882 prohibited Jews from acquiring rural property and expelled them from Moscow. Official quotas were established for Jewish students in secondary schools and universities.

Conditions deteriorated rapidly. By the mid-1880s, fully one-third of Russian Jewry depended upon relief provided by Jewish agencies. The first response to this dire situation was emigration. About 3 million Jews left Eastern Europe between 1881 and 1914. Of these, 2 million settled in the United States. Many others went to Canada, Argentina, and Britain. In addition, a hardy but idealistic few began resettling the ancient homeland of Palestine.

The pogroms and the May Laws gave a powerful impetus to the development of a Zionist sensibility. Many Russian Jews began to realize that they would never truly be safe and secure as a people until they had a home of their own. These ideas first found expression in the Bilu movement.

Over 4 million Jews lived within the Pale. These are the cities where pogroms and anti-Semitic violence occurred during the period of 1871–1906.

The Bilu Movement

After the pogroms of 1881–82, 17 young Russian Jewish students settled in Palestine. These young people, known as Bilu'im, were deeply committed to the Zionist ideal. They labored long, hard hours in the fields under the blazing sun—and they suffered nights of cold, fear, and danger in the new farm settlements.

The Bilu'im took their name from the initials of a four-word passage in the Bible, *Beit Yaakov lekhu venelkhah*, "House of Jacob, let us arise and go" (Isaiah 2:5). They interpreted these words as encouragement to rise up from their diaspora homes and go to Israel to rebuild the Jewish homeland.

A Jewish farm family in Rishon le-Zion reaps the grape harvest. Note the leaf-covered watchtower. During the harvest season, armed Jewish watchmen protected the crops from Arab raiders. The leafy hut on stilts is a sukkah. Ancient Jewish farmers, also stood guard to protect their crops from raiders and built sukkot to shade themselves from the hot sun.

Hovevei Zion

In 1881 Leon Pinsker, a physician, excited Russian Jewry with a pamphlet entitled *Auto-Emancipation.* It caused a great stir, particularly among students and young people. Pinsker maintained that no one could really emancipate the Jews except the Jews themselves. And the only way in which the Jews could secure their freedom and self-respect, he declared, was by returning to their ancient homeland. Pinsker's call gave rise to a society which took the name Hovevei Zion, "Lovers of Zion."

The Hovevei Zion and the Bilu'im founded the first agricultural settlements in the Land of Israel, Rishon le-Zion ("First in Zion") and Petah Tikvah ("Gate of Hope"). Nes Ziyyonah, Zikhron Yaakov, and several others soon followed.

Title page of the original statutes of the Bilu organization. The Hebrew motto means, "The little one shall become a thousand, and the small one a strong nation" (Isaiah 60:22).

The Bilu Pioneers

The pioneers who went to Palestine set themselves a mighty task, but their idealism and comradeship carried them through the arduous beginnings. They found a barren land—dry, rocky, and sandy, with many swampy areas. They saw that the desert would have to be irrigated before vegetables and trees could be planted. Most of the colonists were students and townspeople. What they lacked in knowledge of farming they made up in enthusiasm.

The Jews of Europe followed the progress of the new settlements with keen interest. Wealthy men like Baron Edmond de Rothschild (1845–1934), the French financier and philanthropist, generously contributed much-needed money to buy land and tools.

The settlers worked by day and stood guard at night with their guns, ready to defend themselves against Arab marauders. Their orange groves and olive trees attested to their labors, as did the towns of Rishon le-Zion and Petah Tikvah, which are still the pride of Israel.

The Dreyfus Affair / 1884–1899

French Jewry

The situation of French Jewry in the late 19th century resembled that of German Jewry. Although full civil rights had been extended to them by law, French Jews often found themselves face-to-face with prejudice when they sought to enter certain professions. The old picture of the Jew as a convenient scapegoat could not be wiped out by the enactment of liberal legislation. It was easier to pass laws proclaiming freedom and tolerance than to educate people to abide by their spirit.

Captain Alfred Dreyfus

In October of 1894, Captain Alfred Dreyfus (1859–1935), a Jewish officer on the French general staff, was charged with espionage and arrested. Accused of giving military secrets to Germany, Dreyfus was tried, convicted of high treason, and imprisoned on Devil's Island. To the end, he insisted that he was innocent. When he was stripped of his military rank and honor, he cried, "Long live France! Long live the army!"

Emile Zola

Many people believed that Dreyfus was innocent—framed by anti-Jewish officers who had used forged documents to convict him. Among those who championed the captain's cause was Emile Zola, the great novelist, whose passionate crusade on behalf of Dreyfus was heralded in an essay entitled "J'Accuse," condemning the French government as unjust, intolerant, and corrupt.

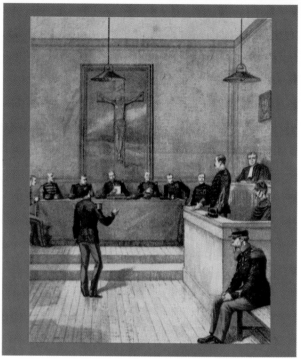

The trial of Captain Dreyfus

Dreyfus Is Pardoned

In time it was found that the real culprit was one Major Ferdinand Esterhazy, who had sold information to the Germans. In 1899 Dreyfus was recalled from Devil's Island and granted a pardon.

Freedom-loving people in many lands had taken part in the fight to prove Dreyfus innocent. His fate had become a

Photograph of part of a letter Dreyfus sent to the chief rabbi of France from prison, the day after he was found guilty.

test case in a much larger struggle then taking place in Europe between those who clung to old prejudices and those who demanded civil rights and equality for all. In 1906 the French government finally admitted that Dreyfus was innocent of all charges and reinstated him in the army.

Theodor Herzl:

The Journalist at the Trial

Among the reporters at the Dreyfus trial in 1894 was Theodor Herzl (1860–1904), a young newspaperman from Vienna. The miscarriage of justice and the degrading treatment to which Dreyfus was subjected made a deep impression on Herzl. Up to that time he had led a fully assimilated life, but when he saw what

Caricature of the four army officers involved in the Dreyfus trial.

harm anti-Semitic hatred could do even in a civilized country like France, he felt himself united in a bond of shared suffering with Dreyfus, the French Jew, and with all of his fellow Jews.

The degradation of Captain Dreyfus

Theodor Herzl

"The Jewish State"

Influenced by the patriotic and nationalist ideas that were so strong in the 19th century, Theodor Herzl conceived a daring solution for the problems the Jews faced in their quest for equal rights. If they established a state of their own, he reasoned, they would once again be a nation like the other nations of the world. No one would be able to victimize or mistreat them. In 1896 Herzl explained his ideas in a book entitled *The Jewish State.*

Herzl soon realized that there was only one possible site for the Jewish state he imagined: Palestine. In 1902, he set forth his vision of the return to Zion in a novel, *Altneuland* ("Old-New Land"). He and his associates, who called themselves Zionists, founded a periodical, *Die Welt* ("The World"), through which to publicize their program.

The Zionist Movement

In 1897 Herzl convened the First Zionist Congress in Basel, Switzerland, inviting Jewish representatives from all over the world who shared his vision. It was at this Congress that the Zionist movement was officially founded and its basic platform proclaimed—the establishment of a legally secure Jewish homeland in Palestine. Herzl became the first president of the World Zionist Organization.

Theodor Herzl dedicated his whole life and energy to the realization of this ideal. Since Palestine was then part of the Turkish Empire, he met with the sultan to obtain permission for Jews to resettle the Holy Land. When the sultan refused, Herzl despairingly approached officials in Egypt and England to see whether he could obtain some territory in East Africa as an alternative site for a Jewish homeland. This idea was soon dropped because of bitter opposition in Zionist circles.

Herzl inflamed the Jews of Europe with the Zionist idea and gave Zionism its basic organizational and political structure. His diplomatic efforts on its behalf won it international standing and recognition. Although he laid the essential groundwork, Theodor Herzl did not live to see even the beginnings of the realization of his plans. He died in 1904 at the age of 44, leaving his associates to continue the work he had begun.

The Gate of Hope

Herzl's most enthusiastic followers did not live in Austria, Germany, or France, but in Russia, where tsar and nobles ruled with a heavy hand, and Jews lived under very oppressive conditions. Herzl opened a gate of hope for many Russian Jewish young people, who looked to Palestine for a life of dignity and freedom.

The land for the first settlements in Palestine was purchased by Keren Kayemet Le-'Yisrael (Jewish National Fund), established in 1901 as the land-purchasing agency of the Zionist movement.

The Jewish National Fund depended on small sums of money collected from Jews throughout the world. The blue-and-white JNF box found a place in millions of Jewish homes.

A Gate of Hope

Zionism After Herzl

After Theodor Herzl's death, David Wolffsohn (1856–1914), one of his close co-workers, took over the leadership of the Zionist Organization. These were stormy days. New and terrible pogroms were taking place in Russia, and many thousands of Jews fled. Most of them made the long journey across the Atlantic and found new homes in the United States. Others went to the countries of Western Europe or to England. Only a few were permitted to enter Palestine. Yet Jewish immigration to the Holy Land continued steadily and a number of new settlements were founded.

The First Aliyah

The Hebrew word *aliyah* (lit. "going up") refers to the ascent to the reader's desk of a person who is called upon to recite blessings during the reading of the Torah. Ever since the time of Ezra, it has also designated the return of Jews to the Land of Israel, both in groups and individually. Each of the five great waves of immigration to Israel in modern times is called an aliyah.

The First Aliyah began in 1880 and continued until 1905. The first *olim* ("ascenders," a noun derived from *aliyah*) were the Bilu'im. Their numbers were reinforced by settlers stimulated by Herzl's writings and the establishment of the World Zionist Organization.

The men and women of the First Aliyah faced an enormous task. They literally had to make the desert bloom again. They began by draining the land's malaria-laden swamps and irrigating its parched, sandy soil. Then they proceeded to plant vineyards and fields. The agricultural settlements they founded, living and working together for the common good, were forerunners of the kibbutzim of later decades.

The Heritage of Enlightenment

The settlers of the First Aliyah brought with them the heritage of the Haskalah. Many of them had studied science, literature, and modern languages at Russia's universities. They began to create new literary works and, most important, made Hebrew—so long used only for prayer and study—come alive again as a spoken, everyday language.

Hashomer, one of the first Jewish self-defense units watchmen in the Galilee (1904). Israel Shohat, its first commander, is in the center of the photo.

In 1909 Tel Aviv was nothing more than a series of sand dunes. This rare old photo shows the allocation of plots of land to the first residents of Tel Aviv.

The Revival of Hebrew

As settlers from many different places arrived in Palestine, the need for a common language became apparent. Some settlers advocated that it be Yiddish or even German, but these tongues were both of European origin, and were unfamiliar to Sephardim and Jews from the Muslim countries. Hebrew was the obvious choice; although not yet suited to modern uses, it was the one language known to most Jews, and had been the language of the Jewish homeland before the exile.

Eliezer Ben-Yehudah (1858-1922), the father of spoken Hebrew.

allowed only Hebrew to be spoken in his home, and his family and friends followed his example. He coined new words for tools and ideas that were unknown to ancient Hebrew. Some years before the outbreak of World War I, he embarked on the monumental task of compiling an unabridged dictionary of the Hebrew language which included the new expressions he had created.

The Haskalah, despite the opposition of some religious leaders, had already introduced the use of Hebrew for secular purposes. The two most ardent champions of the Hebrew revival were Eliezer Ben-Yehudah (1858–1922) and Asher Ginzberg (1856–1927), who called himself Ahad Ha-Am ("One of the People").

Eliezer Ben-Yehudah

Eliezer Ben-Yehudah, considered the father of modern Hebrew, was a talented linguist and educator who foresaw the creative role that Hebrew could play in the everyday life of the new Jewish homeland. Once he arrived in Palestine in 1881, Ben-Yehudah

Ahad Ha-Am

Ahad Ha-Am was the leading essayist in modern Hebrew. He fashioned it into an instrument of precise and articulate expression. Ahad Ha-Am was not a Zionist, and believed that most Jews would continue to live in the diaspora even if a Jewish state was established. Nonetheless, he argued that the Land of Israel must be the spiritual and cultural center of the entire Jewish people. His writings inspired a whole generation of creative Hebrew writers, chief among whom was his close disciple, the poet of the Hebrew national renaissance, Hayim Nahman Bialik (1873–1934).

Hayim Nahman Bialik (1873–1934), the greatest Hebrew poet of modern times. Bialik's first poem was about his longing for Shivat Zion, the Return to Israel. Bialik supported himself as a businessman, teacher, and publisher.
In Israel today, Bialik is considered the national poet, just as Shakespeare is in English-speaking countries.

Israeli poster promoting the study of Hebrew

The Second Aliyah / 1905–1914

The Second Aliyah extended from 1905 until the outbreak of World War I in 1914. This wave of immigration marked the development of a new type of agricultural settlement in Palestine, the kibbutz or cooperative. The members of a kibbutz not only worked and lived together, but actually owned everything jointly. The kibbutz supplied their food, clothing, and other necessities, paying for these goods with the proceeds from the sale of its agricultural products.

A Keren Kayemet poster in Hebrew, Polish, and Yiddish inviting settlers to settle in the valley of Jezreel, in Palestine.

The Jewish National Fund

The land for the settlements was provided by the Keren Kayemet Le-Yisrael, or Jewish National Fund, which was established in 1907 as the land-purchasing agency of the Zionist movement. The JNF was and still is supported by contributions from Jews the world over.

The Histadrut

The pioneers in Palestine organized into a strong federation of labor unions known as the Histadrut Ha-Ovdim ("Federation of Workers"). Eventually the Histadrut evolved into a powerful organization which included all the Jewish working people in the country.

Mounted Shomrim on patrol

Members of the Second Aliyah opposed the practice of hiring Arab laborers to do their field work.

Women stood shoulder to shoulder with the men and shared the back-breaking work in the kibbutzim.

America Beckons

Throughout its history, one country in particular opened its doors to the poor and wronged of all nations and creeds. Indeed, at the very gateway to this land stood a statue, the symbol of liberty, on which were engraved words written by Emma Lazarus (1849–1887), a compassionate and gifted Jewish poet.

Give me your tired, your poor,
Your huddled masses yearning to
breathe free,
The wretched refuse of your teeming
shore,
Send these, the homeless, tempest-tost,
to me.
I lift my lamp beside the golden door!

Polish Jews asking advice about emigrating to the United States at the information desk of the Hebrew Immigrant Aid Society in Warsaw.

In the latter part of the 19th century and the beginning of the 20th, hundreds of thousands of Russian Jews left their homes and sailed to America. Most of them had to make the long journey under difficult conditions, crowded together in the steerage—the most cramped and uncomfortable part of a passenger ship. But they were glad to leave Russia for the land of promise across the Atlantic.

In 1905 a revolution took place in Russia. It was brutally crushed. As in 1881–82, there were bloody pogroms against the Jewish communities. Jews in Europe and America held out a helping hand to the refugees who poured out of Russia. Jewish philanthropists donated generous sums of money, and organizations were formed to aid the immigrants in establishing new homes. Some of them settled in Western Europe or in South America, but most went to the United States.

The Statue of Liberty was a golden door and beacon of hope and freedom for all immigrants.

Front page of the HIAS journal, the *Jewish Immigrant*. The lady is opening the gates of America to the wandering Jew.

Jews in the American Community

About a quarter of a million Jews lived in America in the year 1880. In the next fifty years, two and a half million more came to these shores.

The great majority of this vast influx of immigrants came from Eastern Europe, from lands, including Poland and Lithuania, which were now under Russian rule.

The May Laws

Jews suffered harsh oppression under the government of the tsars. The assassination in 1881 of Tsar Alexander II, who had attempted some reforms, brought on a rapid worsening of their condition. Government-inspired pogroms were followed by the May laws of 1882, which expelled the Jews from many towns and many professions.

The Great Exodus

As hopes for living a good life or improving the lot of their children faded for the Jews of Eastern Europe, a great exodus began. Without funds and with few skills for living in the industrialized Western world, hundreds of thousands crossed the western borders of their homelands, seeking new lands and new opportunities.

Some went to France, Germany, and other West European countries; some to England and to South Africa. A small idealistic group went to Palestine, although they knew that Turkish oppression and the hardships of an undeveloped land awaited them. Baron Maurice de Hirsch, the great philanthropist, aided the emigration from Russia, setting up the Jewish Colonization Association to aid resettlement, particularly in Argentina. The Alliance Israélite Universelle in France, and later the Hilfsverein der Deutschen Juden in Germany, furnished some help. The British Mansion House Committee helped those who arrived in England.

The great majority of those fleeing Old World persecution had no other wish than to go to the land of opportunity, the free country of America. After miserable voyages, usually in the crowded steerage or cheap compartment of the steamships that carried them, these hopeful refugees arrived in the "Golden Land."

Baron Maurice de Hirsch.

Mauricia, Jewish farm colony in Argentina founded by the Jewish Colonization Association of Baron de Hirsch for East European Jews who wished to settle there.

The Love of Learning

Some Jewish immigrants became farmers, encouraged by the Jewish Agricultural Society and the National Farm School, but they were few. For the most part, the newcomers wished to live in cities, in communities where there were many fellow Jews, and where there would be synagogues to attend and religious schools for their children. The shul and the heder, which they had loved in the old country, were transplanted to the new one.

The Jews of Eastern Europe brought with them their love of learning. They managed to find the few dollars necessary to pay the melamed who taught their children Hebrew, Humash, and prayers. They wished in this new country to fashion the life of faith and piety they had known in their small towns in Europe.

Even those who no longer strictly observed Jewish law, and those who devoted themselves to Haskalah or to secularist political movements, had the Jewish love of learning and the printed word. Jewish immigrants published and read more periodicals than any other immigrant group, before or since. They read Yiddish newspapers and Hebrew magazines, and flocked to the Yiddish theater and to public lectures and discussions.

After a day of hard work, many of the adults went to night school to learn English and to qualify to become American citizens. They sacrificed to send their children to high school and, if possible, to college, so that they could do more in life than their parents had been able to do. The ideal profession they wished for their children was one that combined learning and service, such as medicine, law, or teaching.

Helping Each Other

Poor as most of them were, the immigrant Jews never forgot their responsibility to one other. They set up free loan societies, charities, and organizations for fellowship and mutual help. Many belonged to landsmanshaftn—societies made up of immigrants from the same European town.

The old tradition of charity and good deeds was continued in the New World. As poor as an immigrant might be, no home was too crowded to take in a cousin or other relative who had just arrived from the old country.

Jews who were already established in the United States also helped the newcomers. Organizations like B'nai B'rith and the American Jewish Committee, supported largely by German Jews whose parents or grandparents had come to America a few decades earlier, fought anti-Semitism and protected the rights of new immigrants.

Poverty, crowded slum conditions, and unfamiliarity with the lifestyle of the New World were all handicaps for the immigrant. To make the younger people feel at home in America, educational and vocational courses and group social activities were sponsored by the Hebrew Immigrant Aid Society, the National Council of Jewish Women, the Educational Alliance in New York, and the YMHA's and settlement houses.

The Educational Alliance in New York, 1895

The Second Generation

The Jewish Tradition Weakens

The second generation, the children of the immigrants, were able to find better jobs and often to enter professions. In the free atmosphere of America, many of them left the old way of life. They were unwilling to be different from their neighbors, or to lose jobs refusing to work on the Sabbath. Many felt that the religion of their parents was not suited to modern America.

Even the secular culture so dear to some of their parents was often not important to them. They did not attend the Yiddish theater and lecture hall, or read the Yiddish newspapers and magazines of their parents. Their language was English, and they wanted above all to be like other Americans. Some were ashamed of their parents because of their foreign accents or old-fashioned ways.

The Reform Temples

The Reform temples of the late 19th century and the early 20th were not places where the children of East European immigrants could feel at home. Many temples held their Sabbath services on Sunday. Often their members disliked the foreign accents and mannerisms of their East European brethren, and preferred the society of their own kind.

Not respecting their parents' ways, and not welcomed in the Reform temples, young people were all too often growing up detached from Jewish tradition and from the Jewish community.

Jews of all ages reading in the Aguilar Free Library, New York, 1895

Temple Emanuel of New York as it appeared in 1868 at the corner of Fifth Avenue and 43rd Street; it is now located at Fifth Avenue and 65th Street.

Some American boys went to heder, studying Torah the way it had been studied in Europe, for many hours each week.

The First World War / 1914

The Shot Heard Round the World

In 1914 the shot heard round the world sparked off the First World War, in which the Central Powers (Germany, Austria-Hungary, and Turkey) and the Allies (France, Russia, England, and Italy) were pitted against each other in Europe, Africa, and the Middle East.

In each belligerent country Jews fought side by side with their fellow citizens. Many Jewish soldiers died on both sides. When the war began there were more than 500,000 Jews in Germany. More than 100,000 served in the armed forces; 35,000 were decorated for bravery and 12,000 were killed in action.

Most of the major battles of the war were fought in France and Belgium, the western front, and in Poland and Russia, the eastern front. The eastern front stretched along the borders of Russia and through the Pale of Settlement. The war brought great suffering to the Jews in these territories. Most of the able-bodied men served in the Russian army. Many lost their homes. Others were deported because the Russians suspected them of disloyalty. Many Russian Jews were sent deeper into the vast eastern areas of the tsarist empire.

In 1917 the Russian people revolted. The tsar was deposed and executed. The following year, torn by confusion and bloodshed, Russia signed a separate peace treaty with the Central Powers. Civil war broke out in western Russia, with supporters of the new Communist regime fighting an opposition ranging from moderate socialists to advocates of restoring the tsarist monarchy.

Jewish self-defense unit in Odessa, April 1918. This unit was very well-equipped compared to most, as its members had uniforms and even a machine gun.

Jewish soldiers and officers of the Austro-Hungarian army at prayer. Painting by Joseph Ehrenfreund.

The Balfour Declaration / 1917

Chaim Weizmann

One of England's most brilliant chemists, Dr. Chaim Weizmann (1874–1952), was also a leader of the World Zionist Organization. Weizmann, who was born in Russia, settled in England in 1903, where he taught chemistry at the University of Manchester. During World War I, England had to cope with a serious shortage of acetone, a material required for the manufacture of explosives. Weizmann discovered a new formula for acetone, thus making an invaluable contribution to the Allied war effort.

When government officials asked Weizmann to name a price for his discovery, he refused to accept any payment, but asked that Britain allow unrestricted Jewish immigration into Palestine once the war was won. The British agreed, for they knew that the Jewish settlers, having no bonds with Turkey, could be relied upon to help England.

The Balfour Declaration

On November 2, 1917, Arthur James Balfour, the British Foreign Secretary, sent a letter to Lord Walter Rothschild asking him to inform the Zionist Organization of the British government's favorable attitude toward the proposed Jewish national home in Palestine. This letter, which is now known as the Balfour Declaration, brought rejoicing to Zionists the world over.

The Balfour Declaration

The Jewish Legion

In addition to the Jewish soldiers already serving in the British armed forces, all-Jewish fighting units were organized to fight under the blue-and-white Zionist flag. The first of these was the Zion Mule Corps, which served in the Gallipoli campaign in 1915. Its successor, the Jewish Legion, fought under General Edmund Allenby in the campaign to liberate Palestine from the Turks. One of the members of the Jewish Legion was a young immigrant from Russia, David Ben-Gurion, who later became the first Prime Minister of the State of Israel. Another was Vladimir Jabotinsky (1880–1940), the founder of Revisionist Zionism. It was largely thanks to his advocacy that the British agreed to form all-Jewish fighting units.

Vladimir Jabotinsky (1880–1940) in the uniform of the Jewish Legion, which he founded in World War I. Jabotinsky was imprisoned by the British for organizing the Haganah. Later, he founded the Zionist Revisionist movement and the Irgun Zvai Leumi.

After World War I

World War I interrupted the flood of immigration which had increased the number of Jews in the United States to nearly 4 million. Immigrants who had entered the country during the past 33 years made up most of the Jewish population. They had learned how to live in the new land and had established themselves as citizens. Their children were growing up as Americans.

Following the war, when the flow of immigrants resumed, nationalist feelings in the United States were aroused, and resentment against foreigners grew. In 1924 Congress passed the Johnson Act, a restrictive immigration law that established a quota system favoring the Germanic countries and England, and severely limiting immigration from the countries of Southern and Eastern Europe.

The Johnson Act reduced Jewish immigration to several thousand a year. After 1924, with the rate of immigration from Europe curtailed, the problem of preserving Jewish identity in America assumed new forms. The problem was not how to integrate the newcomers into America, but how to raise the native-born American

The new land for some was as poverty stricken as the old. This basement heder, somewhere on Hester Street in the ghetto of New York, was photographed by Jacob Riis.

Jewish citizen to a higher level of Jewish knowledge and awareness.

American Jewry had established its own institutions and was beginning to develop its own leaders and teachers, while the great Jewish communities of Europe faced a period of darkness and destruction.

Painting depicting the stream of numbed immigrants and their back-breaking labor in the sweatshops. Albert Einstein, in front, with the white hair, was one of them.

ALBERT EINSTEIN

Albert Einstein, mathematician and Jew, fled Germany in 1933 and found refuge in the United States. Six years later he sent President Franklin Roosevelt a letter informing him that atomic research in Germany created the possibility that the enemy was making a new kind of super-bomb. Roosevelt took the warning seriously and set up a committee of scientists to develop the atomic bomb. Many Jewish refugee scientists worked on the Manhattan Project. The atomic bomb shortened the war with Japan and saved thousands of American lives. The bomb ushered in the Atomic Age and has been both a blessing and a plague to humanity.

The Palestine Mandate

After the war, the newly formed League of Nations gave Germany's colonies and many former Turkish territories in trusteeship to England and France to be guided and controlled until such time as they would be able to govern themselves. Palestine became a British mandate, and the Balfour Declaration was incorporated into the charter by which it was to be governed. This meant that the League endorsed the principle that Palestine was to become the Jewish homeland. Under the mandate, Hebrew became one of Palestine's three official languages (the other two were English and Arabic).

The Arabs

Many of Palestine's Arab inhabitants opposed the Balfour Declaration and Jewish immigration. Wealthy Arab landowners feared that Jews from Europe would bring in a standard of living much higher than that of the Arab peasants who tilled the soil of Palestine with the same primitive tools as their ancestors centuries earlier, causing them to become discontented with their lot. Arabs marauders were incited to raid Jewish settlements in order to force the Jews to abandon them. But the Jews fought back. They worked their land by day and guarded it at night with their guns.

The British government in 1922 divided the promised Jewish homeland by cutting off three-quarters of the land area of Palestine. A new Arab state was created, called Transjordan. In 1946 Transjordan became independent. It is now called Jordan.

The Third Aliyah

The early years of the British Mandate, 1919 to 1923, marked the period of the Third Aliyah. This wave of immigration consisted mainly of Jews from Poland and Russia.

Lawrence of Arabia (right) arranged a meeting between Emir Feisal (center) and Chaim Weizmann (left). Weizmann traveled by boat and camel to discuss the Palestinian situation with the emir. The two leaders developed a friendly respect for each other's view. They issued a statement agreeing to the recognition of Zionist aims in Palestine if the Arabs were given independence in Syria and Iraq. The territories, which were then ruled by the French and the British, were not given independence and the Jewish-Arab alliance collapsed.

The Jewish Awakening

JEWISH HIGHLIGHTS

The Tsars 19th century	Alexander II 19th century	Haskalah Movement 19th century	Persecution 19th century	The Jewish State 19th-20th century

JEWISH EVENTS • PERSONALITIES • LITERATURE

The Tsars	Alexander II	Haskalah Movement	Persecution	The Jewish State
Kahal abolished	Abolished draft	Hebrew reborn	Pogroms (1881–1884)	Dreyfus convicted Emile Zola
Crown schools	May Laws	Haskalah Abraham Mapu	May laws	Theodor Herzl
Jewish boys drafted	Pogroms / 1881	Judah Leib Gordon	Expulsion from Moscow	First Zionist Congress 1897
	Bilu movement	Yitzhak Ber Levinsohn	School quotas	First Alyah Tel Aviv founded 1909
		Yiddish literature	3 million Jews emigrate	Revival of Hebrew Eliezer Ben-Yehudah Ahad Ha-Am Hayim Nahman Bialik
		Mendele Mokher Seforim	Bilu movement	
		Sholem Aleichem	Leon Pinsker Lovers of Zion	Keven Kayemet Jewish National Fund
		I. L. Peretz	Rishon Le-Zion Petah Tikvah	
			Zikhron Yaakov	

WORLD HISTORY

The Tsars	Alexander II	Haskalah Movement	Persecution	The Jewish State
Tsar Nicholas I	Tsar Alexander II Tsar Liberator Assassination	Russia	Alexander III	Sultan of Turkey
Alexander I		Poland		France
				Major Esterhazy

The Jewish Awakening

JEWISH HIGHLIGHTS

Second Aliyah

Jews in America
20th century

Jewish Organizations
20th century

World War I
1914

JEWISH EVENTS • PERSONALITIES • LITERATURE • HOLIDAYS

Second Aliyah	Jews in America	Jewish Organizations	World War I
Jewish National Fund	Baron Maurice de Hirsch Jewish Colonization Association	B'nai B'rith	Civil War in Russia
Histadruth	Alliance Israélite Universelle	American Jewish Committee	Chaim Weizmann
		Hebrew Immigration Society	Balfour Declaration
		Landsmannschaft	Vladimir Jabotinsky Jewish Legion David Ben-Gurion
		Reform temples	Mandate restrictions
		Johnson Act 1924	Third Aliyah
		Sweatshops Unions Samuel Gompers	

WORLD HISTORY

Basle Switzweland	Tsar Nicholas I	Tsar Liberator Assassination	World War I
	Alexander I		Allenby defeats Turks
			Amir Feisal

Life in the New World

For most of the immigrants, the fulfillment of America's promise was long delayed. The majority of them landed in New York, and great numbers found homes there and in the other large cities of the east. They lived in crowded tenements in neighborhoods like the Lower East Side of New York. Unlike the ghettos of Europe, Jews congregated in these neighborhoods for social and economic reasons, not because of legal restrictions, and those who eventually gained some measure of success were able to move to better areas.

Not knowing English, the immigrants worked at low-paying jobs and were often exploited. The great new industry in the cities was the manufacture of clothing. Many of the newcomers became workers in the garment industry, sewing or tailoring or pressing. Often they worked for 12 or more hours a day, six days a week. In addition, they brought piecework home for the whole family, including the children, to work on till late at night. Even with everyone working, the family's income was very meager.

Samuel Gompers (1850-1924), a British-born Jew who started as a cigar-maker in New York, became founder and president for 38 years of the American Federation of Labor.

Poor conditions at work and at home often led to shortened lives. Tuberculosis claimed many exhausted workers. More dramatically, unsafe conditions led to injuries and to fires which took many lives. When the Triangle Shirtwaist factory in New York burned in 1911, 156 workers were killed, nearly all of them Jewish women. The newcomers were willing to submit to these conditions because of their great need to make a living for themselves and their children.

Driven by a desire to improve working conditions, Jews played a major part in the growth of trade unions in the United States. Samuel Gompers (1850–1924), the founder of the American Federation of Labor, was an immigrant from England. In the early years of the 20th century, East European Jews built up the International Ladies' Garment Workers Union, which fought for shorter hours, safe conditions, and steady pay. By cooperating with the manufacturers when possible, the unions ultimately benefitted them as well.

Fellow Workers!

Join in rendering a last sad tribute of sympathy and affection for the victims of the Triangle Fire. THE FUNERAL PROCESSION will take place Wednesday, April 5th, at 1 P. M. Watch the newspapers for the line of march.

צו דער לויה שוועסטער און ברידער!

A black-bordered circular in three languages (English, Yiddish, Italian) calling upon the people of New York to pay their last respects to the victims of the Triangle Fire. 156 workers, mostly Jews, were killed.

Jewish tradition was observed even amidst the poverty of the ghetto. This poor Jew is preparing for the Sabbath in his cellar home.

The Jewish Theological Seminary

Sabato Morais (1823–1897) and a group of like-minded associates founded the Jewish Theological Seminary of America in 1886 in New York. They hoped that the rabbis ordained there, all of whom were to be English-speaking college graduates, would be able to keep Jewish youth loyal to their heritage. The movement that came into being with the founding of the Seminary is known as Conservative Judaism.

Alexander Kohut (1842–1894), Benjamin Szold (1829–1902), and Marcus Jastrow (1829–1903) were among the scholars who helped fashion this new religious denomination. From the start the Conservatives differed with the Reform movement, upholding loyalty to Torah and Talmud, observance of the Sabbath and dietary laws, Hebrew as the language of prayer, and the preservation of hopes for the return to Zion.

Solomon Schechter

From England's Cambridge University in 1902 came Dr. Solomon Schechter (1847–1915) to head the Seminary. Schechter was a dynamic teacher whose great learning combined East European devotion with modern scholarly discipline. He had become famous for his discovery of the Cairo Genizah, a storehouse of discarded ancient manuscripts that shed much light on Jewish history.

Under Schechter's leadership, the Seminary became a first-rank scholarly institution with an unsurpassed library. The Conservative movement, as Schechter and his associates saw it, was a continuation of the Historical School of Judaism founded by Zechariah Frankel. In the Conservative view, Judaism, like all other human institutions, has developed through the ages, not by sudden reforms but in response to the will and needs of its faithful adherents.

Early photograph of the Jewish Theological Seminary of America in New York.

Solomon Schechter (1847-1915), scholar of Eastern Europe, Germany, and England, called from Cambridge University to head the Jewish Theological Seminary of America in 1902. He gathered the great faculty and library of the Seminary, and gave form to the Conservative movement.

The People of the Book

The Jews are the "people of the book," but they are also the people of the magazines, newspapers, and periodicals. Wherever Jews have set roots, even temporarily, some enterprising intellectuals always found reason to publish a newspaper or magazine.

The Yiddish-speaking masses in the major U.S. cities, not yet fluent in English, created a cultural life of their own which helped them to adjust to their new and difficult environment. Hundreds of newspapers, magazines, and periodicals in Yiddish, Hebrew, German, Ladino, Russian, Polish, Hungarian, and other languages appeared to offer guidance, news, entertainment, and advice for a generation struggling to accommodate itself to a new world. In particular the Yiddish press served these ends.

The Jewish Press in the 1900s

In the early 1900s the Jewish press in the United States included over 200 periodicals, 147 in English, 27 in Yiddish, and 11 in Hebrew. The 5 daily Yiddish newspapers had a combined circulation of over 300,000 copies. There were 69 weeklies which provided news of Jewish life throughout the world and furnished forums for discussion.

With the modernization of the Jewish people, there was a flowering of Yiddish literature in Europe and in England, Canada, France, Argentina, and the United States. Besides being a spoken tongue, Yiddish now became the language of books, newspapers, theatrical productions, and political activism. It became the first and also the second language of two-thirds of the Jewish people.

The Jewish Daily Forward

In its heyday, the *Jewish Daily Forward* (*Yiddish Forvets*) was the most widely read Yiddish newspaper in the United States. Its 11 regional editions reached as far as Chicago and had a peak circulation of 200,000.

Abraham Cahan (1860–1951) edited the *Forward* from 1903 to 1951, combining a commitment to good journalism with a belief in the Jewish labor movement. The *Forward* published stories, serialized novels, gave English lessons, and kept the immigrants in touch with local and world events. Its most famous feature was the Bintel Brief, a "Dear Abby"–style advice column which counseled readers on their domestic, personal, and business problems.

The front page of the first issue of the *Jewish Daily Forward*, Wednesday, September 8, 1897. At that time the price of a newspaper was one cent.

The front page of the first Jewish daily in the United States, April 6, 1883.

Front page of the English edition of the *Forward* of July 5, 1996. Inflation has raised the price of the newpaper from one cent to one dollar.

As the pace of immigration fell, the *Forward*'s readership dwindled. By 1970 it had fallen to 44,000. The Yiddish edition of the *Forward* ceased daily publication in 1983 and became a weekly. In 1990 a weekly English edition of the *Forward* made its debut. In 1995 a Russian edition was introduced.

Abraham Cahan, the editor of the *Jewish Daily Foward.*

The Boston Blat

In 1913 a Boston printer named Joseph J. Shore felt the call to provide a newspaper that would serve the Jewish communities of New England. His weekly paper, the *Boston Blat,* was mostly in Yiddish, but because he wisely saw the need to serve a wider audience, it included columns in Hebrew and English.

Undercapitalized, the *Boston Blat* folded its pages after six years of struggle. This typical startup and failure was common among the early newspapers. The renaissance of Hebrew, the Holocaust, and other social changes sent Yiddish into decline.

Yiddish Today

As the search for ethnic identity grows, interest in Yiddish continues to increase. Yiddish courses are becoming common on college campuses. The Yivo Institute for Jewish Research and the Workmen's Circle have published Yiddish textbooks for beginners. The National Yiddish Book Center is building a $5 million complex in Amherst, Massachusetts, and is cataloguing thousands of Yiddish books.

In the Hasidic community, Yiddish is an everyday, living, working, studying, singing tool. Children study their lessons in Yiddish, mothers sing Yiddish lullabies, merchants do business and advertise in Yiddish, and Hasidic comedians (*badchanim*) tell jokes in Yiddish.

Joseph J. Shore, printer and publisher of the *Boston Blat.* He was also an accomplished artist and woodcarver. Shore often carved the large-size Hebrew type for *Boston Blat*'s headlines.

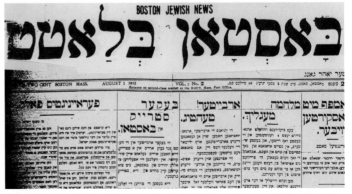

The *Boston Blat,* August 1, 1913. Price, 2 cents. The *Boston Blat—Boston Jewish News* was edited by Joseph J. Shore.

Jewish Public Servants

By the year 1900 there were a million Jews in America. Many, mostly descendants of immigrants who had arrived in the first part of the 19th century, had attained prosperity and status. Among them were well-known public servants and philanthropists, whose activities and charities benefited many others besides their own people.

Oscar Straus (1850–1926) was appointed envoy to Turkey by Grover Cleveland and three Presidents after him, and served in the cabinet of Theodore Roosevelt as Secretary of Commerce and Labor. His brothers Nathan (1848–1931) and Isidor Straus (1845–1912), owners of Macy's in New York, were known for their good deeds. Isidor, at one time a Congressman, was president of the Educational Alliance. Nathan brought about the compulsory pasteurization of milk in New York, and gave generously for health clinics in Palestine in response to an appeal from Henrietta Szold (1860–1945), the founder of Hadassah.

Julius Rosenwald (1862–1932), of Sears Roebuck, gave tremendous sums for many philanthropic causes, including the higher education of blacks. Others who supported learning through their activity and contributions were Judge Mayer Sulzberger (1843–1923) of the Court of Common Pleas in Philadelphia, who was one of the founders of the Jewish Theological Seminary, and his cousin Cyrus L. Sulzberger, president of the Jewish Agricultural Society.

Louis Marshall (1856–1929), outstanding attorney and civic leader, founded the American Jewish Committee and worked for Jewish minority rights at the Versailles Conference after World War I. Though not a Zionist, he supported the building of Palestine as a Jewish refuge. Jacob H. Schiff (1847–1920) worked with him on many projects and helped persuade the U.S. government to censure Russia for its mistreatment of Jews. Schiff was perhaps the outstanding patron of learning of the time, giving funds to institutions ranging from Harvard and Barnard to the Jewish Theological Seminary and the Haifa Technion.

David Sarnoff (1891–1971) began as a messenger boy and wireless operator. He rose to become head of RCA. He was active on behalf of Jewish causes.

Louis Dembitz Brandeis (1856-1941), justice of the Supreme Court and Zionist leader. A champion of liberal causes, he became interested in Judaism and Zionism when he met Jewish garment workers during settlement of a strike in 1910. He said that following Jewish ideals made one a better American.

Jacob H. Schiff (1847–1920), outstanding Jewish philanthropist, gave support to universities, hospitals, and cultural activities both Jewish and general, helping religious institutions of all groups. His firm would not lend money to tsarist Russia because of its persecution of the Jews.

Orthodox Jewry

The leading rabbis and congregations at the turn of the century, as well as the leading philanthropists, were mostly in the Reform wing of Judaism. Rabbis Kaufmann Kohler (1843–1926), Emil Hirsch (1851–1923), David Philipson (1862–1949), and Henry Berkowitz (1857–1924) were among the leaders of Jewish religious life. Conservative and Orthodox rabbis and congregations were not as yet well-organized.

Yeshiva University in New York, an Orthodox institution which includes high schools, undergraduate colleges for men and women, graduate and medical schools, and a rabbinical seminary.

The great majority of Jewish immigrants from 1881 on were Orthodox in background. They attempted to set up the same type of communities as had served them in their former homes. Each congregation, following Jewish tradition and the customs of its members, felt it could stand by itself without looking toward a central authority.

A group of Orthodox Jews in New York City made an attempt to attain unity under the leadership of Rabbi Jacob Joseph (1848–1902), whom they brought from Vilna in Lithuania to be the city's chief rabbi. He proved unable to bring order to New York's teeming Jewish community because most of its Orthodox leaders refused to accept his authority. In Chicago a similar attempt failed.

Umbrella organizations met with more success. In 1898, the Union of Orthodox Jewish Congregations was founded, thanks to the efforts of Rabbi H. Pereira Mendes (1852–1937) of the Shearith Israel Congregation

Dr. Norman Lamm, 1996

in New York. A group of Orthodox rabbis joined together to form the Agudas Harabonim in 1902. One of their aims was to aid academies of learning, yeshivot, both in America and abroad.

Yeshiva University

The outstanding yeshiva in the New World was founded in 1896. Named for a great European scholar, Rabbi Isaac Elchanan, this New York institution began as a rabbinical seminary for students who had already steeped themselves in Jewish learning in European academies. Over the years it expanded into a complete university. Under the presidency of Rabbi Bernard Dov Revel (1885–1940) and his successor, Dr. Samuel Belkin (1911–1976) it grew to include a high school, an undergraduate college, and a variety of graduate and professional schools, including the Albert Einstein Medical School, the Benjamin Cardozo Law School, Stern College for Women, the Sy Sims School of Business, and the Wurzweiler School of Social Work. Under Belkin's successor, Rabbi Norman Lamm (b. 1927), Yeshiva continued to grow. In the 1990s it had 5,200 undergraduate and graduate students, an additional 1,000 students at the affiliates, and an annual operating budget of $350 million.

Anti-Semitism

In the democratic climate of America, Jews found themselves accepted, as they had never been elsewhere, as first-class citizens and productive members of society. Still, anti-Semitism all too often made itself felt even on these shores. In the early part of the 19th century, several states did not grant full legal rights to Jews. Later on, the Know-Nothing party, populist agitators of various stripes, and the Ku Klux Klan aroused feelings against foreigners and minority groups, primarily Catholics and Jews.

Polite Anti-Semitism

"Polite" anti-Semitism, which meant the exclusion of Jews from high society and the refusal to sell them homes in certain areas, was always known to exist. In a famous case in 1877, a hotel in Saratoga, New York, refused to accept Joseph Seligman (1819–1880), a prominent Jewish banker who had been a friend of Presidents Lincoln and Grant, as a paying guest, informing him bluntly that "no Israelite shall be permitted to stop in the hotel." Public opinion was outraged by this incident, but it was not until several decades later that restrictive practices of this kind were outlawed.

More seriously, the great influx of Jewish immigrants and the growth of European anti-Semitism triggered anti-Jewish sentiments among many Americans around the turn of the century. Hatred aroused knows no rhyme or reason. At one and the same time Jews were accused of running the government and of seeking to overthrow it; of being wretchedly poor and fabulously rich; of sticking clannishly to themselves and of trying to break into society. In September 1928, the medieval blood-libel accusation came to life for a brief moment when state troopers in Massena, New York, searching for a missing child who turned out to have been lost in the woods, questioned the local rabbi about reports that Jews offered human sacrifices on Yom Kippur.

The problems Jews experienced in the United States, however troubling, did not compare, either in frequency or in seriousness, with the persecutions and pogroms to which they were subjected in Europe and the Near East. Moreover, the Jews of America stood up for their rights.

Equality for All

From the very beginning, American Jews demanded that they be treated the same as everyone else. In the 19th century they successfully fought against restrictive voting laws. They lobbied the government to take action at the time of the blood-libel of Damascus in 1840. They protested to President Millard P. Fillmore about the restrictions imposed on Jews by Switzerland. They similarly protested, with the support of Protestant leaders, at the time of the Mortara case. And in 1859 they established the Board of Delegates of American Israelites to defend Jewish rights. In 1913 they founded the Anti-Defamation League of B'nai B'rith to combat anti-Semitic libels and protect the civil rights of Jews and other minorities.

The Dreyfus Affair in 1894 aroused widespread concern among all who loved justice, Jews and non-Jews alike. The Kishinev pogrom of 1903 and the wave of pogroms in 1905 were followed by mass demonstrations and protests throughout the civilized world. Congress passed a unanimous resolution expressing American horror at the incidents. Oscar Straus and Jacob Schiff headed a committee which raised $1 million to help the survivors.

The American Jewish Committee

Because of the need for a national organization to safeguard Jewish rights, the American Jewish Committee came into being in 1906. Louis Marshall, the Sulzbergers, Judge Julian Mack, and Rabbi Judah Magnes (1877–1948) were among the founders of this body, whose objectives were "to prevent the infraction of the civil and religious rights of the Jews in any part of the world; to render all lawful assistance; to secure for Jews equality of economic, social and educational opportunity; and to afford relief from calamities affecting Jews, wherever they may occur."

The AJC encouraged the organization of the 1.5 million Jews of New York City into a Kehillah, or communal organization, which was to regulate Jewish law, settle disputes, protect civil rights, and further education. The Kehillah came into being in 1908 and continued in existence for ten years, under the chairmanship of Rabbi Magnes, who later became president of the Hebrew University of Jerusalem. Like most other attempts at Jewish unity, the Kehillah soon came to an end, but its legacy included the New York Bureau of Jewish Education, a model agency imitated in many other cities.

The AJC was active in a long campaign to prevent discrimination by Russia against Jews. Though it spoke for American Jewry, it was initially strongly anti-Zionist, reflecting the Reform ideology of most of its founders.

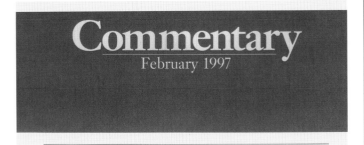

Commentary
February 1997

On the Future of Conservatism
A Symposium

Robert L. Bartley • Peter L. Berger • Walter Berns • William F. Buckley, Jr. Midge Decter • David Frum • Francis Fukuyama • Mark Helprin Gertrude Himmelfarb • William Kristol • Michael Novak • Norman Podhoretz Irwin M. Stelzer • George Weigel • Ruth R. Wisse

The cover page of *Commentary Magazine*, dated May 1996. *Commentary* is one of the leading journals of political thought, published by the American Jewish Committee.

Julian Mack

American Jewish Committee delegation in 1911. *From left to right:* Louis Marshall, Harry Friedenwald, Judge Mayer Sulzberger, Harry Cutler, Oscar S. Straus, Judge Leon Sanders, Henry N. Goldfogle, Samuel Dorf, Leon Kaminsky.

American Zionism

Many Americans, Christians as well as Jews, looked forward to the prophetic return of Jews to the Land of Israel. In 1852, Warder Cresson of Philadelphia converted to Judaism and, bearing the new name of Michael Boaz Israel, tried to establish a Jewish colony near Jerusalem. Clorinda S. Minor of Philadelphia led a Christian group to a settlement called Mount Hope near the site where Tel Aviv was later built.

Emma Lazarus looked forward to a revival of the Jewish national spirit and a rebuilt homeland. Immigrants from Eastern Europe brought the Hovevei Zion movement to the United States, setting up chapters in New York, Boston, and other cities in the 1880s.

Only a token delegation from America attended the First Zionist Congress, convened by Theodor Herzl in Basel in 1897. Yet the Zionist movement in the United States was steadily growing. In 1898 nearly 100 small Zionist clubs united into the Federation of American Zionists, which in 1917 became the Zionist Organization of America.

The rank-and-file members of America's Zionist movement were largely of East European origin, but the leaders included some outstanding Reform rabbis, among them Bernhard Felsenthal (1822–1908), Gustav Gottheil (1827–1903), and Maximilian Heller (1860–1924), who opposed the Reform doctrine that Jews must remain dispersed throughout the world in order to fulfill the "mission of Israel." True fulfillment would come, they felt, when a Jewish model state was allowed to flourish in Palestine.

The Zionist Federation's first secretary was Stephen S. Wise (1874–1949), a Reform rabbi already known for his fiery oratory.

Left to right: Rabbi Stephen S. Wise, Rabbi Israel Goldstein, Louis Lipsky

During World War II he was to become American Jewry's outstanding spokesman to the conscience of the world.

Many American Jews opposed Zionism, arguing that loyalty to America required them to forsake all interest in a Jewish national homeland. The strongest statement of the compatibility of Zionism with loyalty to America came from Louis Dembitz Brandeis (1856–1941), who in 1916 was appointed to the Supreme Court of the United States. "The ideals of the 20th century," he said, "have been Jewish ideals for 20 centuries. To be good Americans, we must be better Jews, and to be better Jews we must become Zionists."

Among the other leading figures in early American Zionism were Henrietta Szold (1860–1945) and Louis Lipsky (1876–1963). Szold, a rabbi's daughter, scholar, and editor of the Jewish Publication Society, founded Hadassah, the women's Zionist organization, in 1912. Lipsky founded America's first English-language Zionist periodical, the *Maccabean*, and was its editor for many years.

The Peace Conference / 1919

After World War I, the victorious nations were anxious to establish a lasting peace and better conditions in the postwar world. The face of Europe had changed. Germany and Austria had lost their empires and become republics. Russia had become a Communist dictatorship. France, although a victor in the great conflict, was exhausted, ravaged by the many bloody battles fought on her soil.

The Peace of Versailles

At the great peace conference at Versailles in 1919, many countries that had been part of the Russian, German, or Austrian empire before the war gained their independence. Poland, Finland, Estonia, Latvia, and Lithuania became independent countries, as did Hungary and Czechoslovakia. Germany lost its African colonies, and in the Middle East, Palestine and Iraq, formerly part of the Ottoman Empire, became British mandates, while Syria became a French mandate.

President Woodrow Wilson was instrumental in creating the League of Nations, an international organization which was to be responsible for maintaining peace in the world. The League supervised the administration of the mandates, including Palestine.

Attending the Versailles Peace Conference, along with the representatives of both the conquered and the conquering lands, were delegates from the many nations that were about to win independence or to gain mandatory status. Also present were Jewish delegations from many countries. American Jewry was represented by Louis Marshall and Judge Mack, among others. Marshall succeeded in uniting all the Jewish delegations to speak with one voice on behalf of the rights not only of Jews but of all minority groups.

The League of Nations

Guarantees of minority rights were included in the treaties negotiated at the Versailles Peace Conference and in the constitutions of the new states that came into existence after the war. The League of Nations was the guardian of the rights of minority groups, but in the years that followed was unable to enforce them, for it had no concrete powers.

At the peace conference Woodrow Wilson exercised a dominating influence. In this painting by William Orpen, he is sitting third from the left. Wilson's Fourteen Points were a summary of America's mission—the extension of self-government and democracy to the whole world.

The Jews of Poland

After World War I, the newly established state of Poland had a Jewish community of 3.3 million, the largest and one of the oldest in Europe and the second-largest in the world. Since Jews were regarded as members of a distinct nationality protected by the minority guarantees laid down at Versailles, Polish Jewry was organized as a Kehillah, with autonomy on the local level. The Kehillah organization owned all communal property, such as synagogues, cemeteries, and hospitals, and ran the community's educational, religious, and social-cultural institutions. The members of the ruling council of the Kehillah were elected by the Jews of each town by direct, secret ballot.

A typical heder in the city of Vilna, part of Poland until World War II, now part of Lithuania.

The Educational System

The greatest achievement of Polish Jewry was its educational system, maintained at its own cost. The different ideological and religious movements all had their own schools. Of the total Jewish school-age population of 425,000, some 340,000 attended these schools. The Jewish community also maintained teacher-training schools, rabbinical academies, trade schools, and other cultural institutions, such as museums, libraries, and adult study courses.

In secular higher education, Jewish students were greatly handicapped because of prejudice against them. As many as half of the Polish Jews who attended universities had to do so in other countries.

Jewish Cultural Life

The cultural life of Polish Jewry, both religious and secular, flourished. There was a large output of books, magazines, newspapers, and other publications. Institutions of higher Jewish learning, such as the famous yeshivot of Lublin and Mir, the Yivo Institute for Jewish Research (in Vilna), and the Institute for the Science of Judaism (in Warsaw), produced well-trained graduates who later spread Jewish knowledge throughout the world.

The Jews of Poland observed Sabbaths and holidays in an atmosphere that glowed with joy and piety. Communal life abounded with a variety of political, social, philanthropic, and mutual aid organizations and institutions which helped Polish Jews cope with the many complex problems that called for action.

Jews also contributed their full measure to the general culture of Poland in science, art, literature, and music.

The Jewish community of Poland functioned under tremendous hardships of financial limitations and governmental discrimination, which drove large many into poverty and emigration. The anti-Semitism of the government and the populace at large produced economic boycotts and outbreaks of violence against Jews. Nevertheless, the Jews of Poland fought for survival with the aid of American Jewry.

Jewish War Victims

The Jews of Western Europe did not regard themselves as minorities, for they had achieved complete emancipation. But the Jews in the many newly-created countries of Central and Eastern Europe were in need of protection. Despite the minority rights guarantees, they were still victims of discrimination. The only country to fully recognize their rights was the new Republic of Czechoslovakia. For several years (1918–24), Jews were granted national autonomy in Lithuania.

The territories of the Ukraine and eastern Poland had been ravaged by heavy fighting during World War I. After the war they remained a battleground, first between the Communist government of Russia and its opponents, then between Russia and Poland. In all of these conflicts, the Jews of the region suffered grievously. Tens of thousands were killed in bloody massacres; the survivors faced the problems of poverty, disease, and homelessness.

The Joint Distribution Committee

The Jews of the United States, aware of the desperate plight of their brethren across the sea, were anxious to help. Although many American Jews were poor, they contributed vast sums of money—in 1917 alone, more than $10 million. To further the relief effort, American Jewry's charitable and relief organizations consolidated into one vast body, the American Jewish Joint Distribution

Some of the founders of the Joint Distribution Committee. Seated at the left is Felix M. Warburg, philanthropist and first JDC chairman.

Committee, generally known as the JDC or the Joint. Its aim was to bring quick, effective assistance to the Jews of Russia and Poland. In addition to providing food, clothing, tools, and medicine, it would, whenever possible, help them to emigrate to other countries.

The American Jewish Congress

During World War I American Jewry was concerned about the status of the Jews of Eastern Europe. In 1918 it set up the American Jewish Congress to protect their rights. Judge Julian W. Mack was chosen president. Harry Friedenwald and Henrietta Szold, ardent Zionists, were among the vice-presidents.

The American Jewish Congress sent a delegation to the postwar peace conferences to demand recognition of Jewish rights and fulfillment of the Balfour Declaration. At the San Remo Conference it successfully lobbied for Britain to be given the Palestine mandate, with the purpose of bringing about a Jewish state.

Country	Number of Jews
Germany	250,00
England	150,000
France	50,000
Belgium, Holland, Spain, etc.	50,000
Poland, Russia, Rumania, Hungary, etc.	2,400,000
	2,900,000

Table showing the origins of Jewish immigrants to the United States up to 1922.

Jews of The Soviet Russia

Despite the huge emigration from Russia in the preceding few decades, about 2.5 million Jews remained in the Soviet Union when the war ended. They were faced with a completely new situation. On the one hand, anti-Semitism was officially outlawed. On the other, Jews were required to give up their religion and culture to become part of the new Communist order. Some Russian Jews were able to adjust to the new life, but many found it impossible to abandon their traditional way of life, language, and religion.

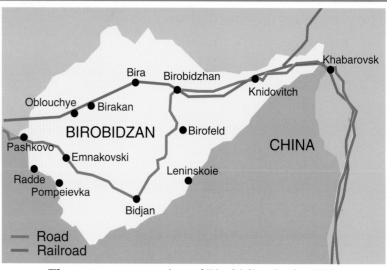

The autonomous region of Birobidjan in the 1930s

Birobidjan

The Soviet government decided to settle the Yiddish-speaking Jews in Birobidjan, a remote area in southeastern Siberia near the Manchurian border, where they could engage in farming. But life in Birobidjan turned out to be very disappointing for those who accepted the offer and settled there.

The Communist Way

The Jews of the Soviet Union hoped that they would be given all the rights of citizenship, including the freedom to preserve their religious and cultural heritage. The Communists, however, were determined to forge a new Russia with only one way of living—the Communist way. And so once again the Jews of Russia found themselves outside the accepted order. Zionists and religious leaders were declared enemies of the regime and arrested. Many Jews who had fought in the Russian Revolution came to view the new system with bitterness and disappointment. Yet for several decades many Soviet Jews continued to hope that life would improve under the new order. Their final disillusionment was not to come until after another world war even more terrible than the first.

Entrance to a collective farm in Birobidjan

A street in the city of Birobidjan

Jewish Problems and Sucesses

JEWISH HIGHLIGHTS

People of the Book The Jewish Press	Jewish Institutions and People	American Zionism	Peace Conference 1919	Eastern Europe 19th century

JEWISH EVENTS • PERSONALITIES • LITERATURE

Jewish Daily Forward Abraham Cahan	American Federation of Labor Samuel Gompers	First Zionist Congress Bernard Felsenthol Gustav Gotthel	Peace of Versailles Louis Marshall	Poland Kehillah Educational system Yeshiva of Lublin Yeshiva of Mir
The *Boston Blat* Joseph J. Shore	Jewish Theological Seminary Solomon Schechter	Rabbi Stephen S. Wise	American Jewish Joint Distribution Committee	Russian Jewish cultural life Birobidjan
	Jewish personalities Louis Dembitz Brandeis Julius Rosenwald Oscar Strauss Jacob H. Schiff David Sarnoff Jacob Joseph	Henrietta Szold Hadassah	American Jewish Congress	Jewish war victims
		Louis Lipsky The *Maccabean*	Jewish leaders	Joint Distribution Committee
	Yeshiva Universiy Rabbi Norman Lamm Rabbi H. Pereira Mendes		Cyrus Adler	American Jewish Committee
	Anti-Semitism Joseph Seligman Blood-libel of Damascus		Meir Berlin	
	American Jewish Committee Julian Mack		Leo Jung	

WORLD HISTORY

Boston	USA	Basel	League of Nations Woodrow Wilson	Poland
New York				Russia

The Jews In Pre-Nazi Germany

After World War I, Germany became a republic. Many Jews played an important role in its political life. The most prominent of them was Walther Rathenau (1867–1922), one of the great statesmen of his time. As Minister of Reconstruction, and later Minister of Foreign Affairs, Rathenau made every effort to improve relations between Germany and France. But reactionary German forces opposed Rathenau, and he was assassinated in 1922.

Members of the German general staff and Adolf Hitler.

The Weimar Republic

Germany's postwar government was known as the Weimar Republic. In the early 1920s Jews became prominent in the arts, sciences, education, banking, and business. For a time it seemed as if the forces of progress would triumph. The Weimar Republic struggled valiantly to solve its problems but was hampered by nationalist military organizations. Their members, yearning for the "good old days," were unable to accept the fact that Germany had been defeated in the war.

Fascism in Italy

In Italy, too, many dreamed of a powerful military regime. In 1922 the Fascist Party, headed by Benito Mussolini, who called himself Il Duce ("The Leader"), seized power. The Fascists were extreme nationalists. Everyone who did not agree with them was conveniently silenced—by imprisonment; many opponents were tortured and put to death.

Hitler and "Mein Kampf"

The German General Staff was not destroyed by the war. It just changed its name. In a short time, even though the postwar treaties forbade such weapons, German officers had made arrangements to manufacture tanks, aircraft, and even poison gas.

By 1919, all of Europe was in a deep economic depression. Millions of unemployed Germans were looking for work. This was fertile ground for the evil genius of Adolf Hitler.

Hitler had been a corporal in World War I and won an Iron Cross for bravery. After the war, he became the leader of a small political organization, the Nazi Party. In 1923, he attempted to overthrow the German government. Tried and convicted, Hitler spent nine months in jail, where he wrote the book *Mein Kampf* ("My Struggle").

No one should have been surprised by the political program Hitler adopted when he came to power, for it was detailed in *Mein Kampf.* But no one took him seriously, and few bothered to read his book.

Anti-Jewish poster issued by the Minister of Propaganda, Berlin, in 1940, with the slogan "Behind the enemy, the Jew" and in French from 1942, with the slogan "And behind the Jew."

Adolf Hitler and Nazism

A new kind of fascism now developed in Germany. In addition to the militarists, there were many other groups that disliked the Weimar government. Many were bitter about Germany's defeat in the war and its loss of territories and prestige. These groups, which fought the democratic builders of the new Germany, eventually found a leader in Adolf Hitler.

Hitler promised the disappointed groups a different, powerful Germany—a Germany that would conquer the world and become an empire such as it had been under the Kaiser; indeed, he promised to make Germany even greater than it had been before.

The Nazis expounded the notion that the German people were a "master race," superior to all others. They and the other "Nordic" peoples, so the Nazis declared, were the master race of mankind which would lead and dominate the world and wipe out all inferior peoples.

Hitler's ideas were not taken seriously in other countries. Even many Germans laughed at them. Nevertheless, Hitler succeeded in winning more and more followers who were blindly devoted to their leader and his ideas.

The Nazi Rise to Power

Throughout the 1920s, the Nazis slowly gained in strength. But it was not until the late 1920s, which saw the combination of a decaying economic order and financial backing from some wealthy industrialists, that the party gained significant popular support. Hitler received funds from Fritz Thiessen of the German steel trust, Emil Kidorf of the German coal industry, and other wealthy businessmen.

In the Reichstag elections of 1928, the Nazis won about 800,000 votes and 12 seats. By 1930, the Nazis had gained over 6 million votes and 107 seats. In 1932, the Nazis received almost 14 million votes, 120 seats, and became Germany's largest political party.

Stormtroopers

Following the example of Mussolini in Italy, the Nazi Party set up a quasi-military unit called the SA, or stormtroopers, to terrorize its opponents and disrupt their political activities. Dressed in military uniforms, trained like soldiers, the stormtroopers marched through the streets, shouting, singing, and breaking up orderly meetings of democratic groups. They started fights and made trouble. In addition to the SA, an elite group called the SS was organized to protect party leaders and maintain discipline among the members.

Racist attitudes in Germany developed from the idea that the Aryan-Nordic race was superior to all other races. To the Nazis, the Teuton stood for goodness, strength, courage, and beauty. Although the Aryan myth existed prior to the Nazis, they turned it into a reality which was readily applied to society.

Hitler Assumes Power

The Great Depression of the 1930s caused great suffering throughout the Western world. Many Germans were unemployed and desperate. During the years of the Depression, Hitler's following increased rapidly.

The Nazis in Power

In 1933, Adolf Hitler came into power, marking the end of the Weimar Republic. The Nazis took over the country. All democratic organizations were systematically dissolved. Germany was in the hands of uniformed men, the SA and the SS. The people were forced to spend their time in military parades and demonstrations to show their loyalty to Hitler—their Fuehrer, or "Leader."

The German people adored the tramp of massed men, the music of military bands, the waving of banners and the conquering songs of thousands. Hitler catered to this feeling, and in a short time, the Germans were ready for a war of conquest.

Behind this masquerade of zeal and devotion the Nazis conducted a reign of terror. Aided by the police, Hitler's stormtroopers made thousands of arrests. No man or woman who had a different point of view or refused to support the new Nazi regime was safe.

Germany: Land of Fear

Germany became a land of fear. People whispered stories of a new kind of prison—the

Adolf Hitler

Nazi stormtroopers gathering Jewish books for destruction.

concentration camp. In Hitler's first years of power, the Nazi concentration camps were filled mostly with political opponents. But from the very beginning Hitler declared war on the Jews. He used them as a scapegoat, inciting latent anti-Semitic prejudices. Cruelties against Jews were encouraged, and one humiliating restriction after another was imposed upon them.

Hitler's main ambition was to forge a Germany that would follow him blindly into a great, victorious war. All obstacles hindering the unity and mindless obedience of such a Germany had to be removed. The German people became afraid to speak freely, even to think. German history was shamelessly rewritten in accordance with the new Nazi viewpoint. Many respected educators and scientists were removed from their posts and replaced by loyal Nazis. The new replacements did as they were told, and helped fashion a Germany that would follow Hitler to war.

More and more Jews were subjected to restrictions. Jewish lawyers, physicians, teachers, scientists, journalists, and actors lost their jobs. Jewish places of business were boycotted by Hitler's party troops and stormed by angry mobs. Jews were insulted publicly and physically attacked.

The 1936 Summer Olympics

In the spring of 1936, Hitler with no opposition, carried out the military occupation of the demilitarized Rhineland. In the summer of that year Berlin was the host city to the Olympic Games. The foreign visitors were impressed with the friendliness of the Germans and enjoyed the red carpet hospitality of the Third Reich.

Behind the Scenes
Everything was open to the visitors except the torture chambers of the stormtroopers and the misery of the concentration camps. The Hollywood facade was wonderful. But behind the scenes, the Nazis refused to allow Jewish athletes to compete for Germany. Gretel Bergmann, a high jumper, and Bruno Lampert, a long jumper, were purposely left off the German team.

The Olympic Games
The opening ceremony at Olympic Stadium in Berlin was reviewed by Hitler, and cheers greeted the teams that dipped their colors and saluted Nazi-style. All other athletes were acknowledged only with silence from the crowd.

The American Controversy
The anti-Semitic and anti-black policies of Adolf Hitler had created a controversy in the United States. Avery Brundage, head of the American Olympic Committee, had urged that the United States should participate in the Berlin games. Judge Jeremiah T. Mahoney, a Catholic and president of the Amateur Athletic Union, argued for a boycott by which no American team would be sent to represent the United States.

Brundage claimed that the boycott plan was a Jewish-Communist conspiracy. He was able to defeat the resolution calling for a boycott. Mahoney resigned as AAU president, and Brundage succeeded him becoming the head of both the AAU and the AOC.

The American Track Team
The American track team included 10 black athletes. The German newspapers called them "the black auxiliary," and printed stories which degraded them. Cornelius Johnson, a black athlete, achieved a record leap in the high jump. Hitler had personally congratulated the first two track and field winners, but he deliberately snubbed Johnson by leaving his box in the stadium.

The blacks on the American track and field team won eight gold medals, three silver medals, and two bronze medals outscoring every national track and field team. Jesse Owens, grandson of slaves, won four gold medals.

Another political incident took place when two American Jewish runners, Marty Glickman and Sam Stoller, were dropped from the 400-meter relay team by coach Dean Cromwell.

The 1936 Berlin games will always be remembered as the "Nazi Olympics." Stormtroopers swastikas, anti-black and anti-Semitic propaganda destroyed what should have been the non-political competition of the Olympics.

Jesse Owens shatters records, showing what "non-Aryan" athletes can do.

Kristallnacht / 1938

In 1935 the German Reichstag passed the so-called Nuremberg Laws, which deprived Germany's Jews of citizenship and officially demoted them to an inferior status. During the next several years, Jewish businesses, homes, and property were expropriated.

On November 9, 1938, the Nazis staged a nationwide terror action that became known as Kristallnacht ("Crystal Night") because of the many broken windows.

Hundreds of synagogues in Germany and Austria were set afire, and about 10,000 Jewish businesses were destroyed and looted. Fifty Jews were murdered by organized mobs of bloodthirsty Nazis.

The excuse for this outrage was the assassination of a German diplomat, Ernst vom Rath, by Herschel Grynszpan, son of Jewish refugees.

Grynszpan, in Paris, had received a letter from his sister in which she stated that the Grynszpan family, together with all Polish Jews living in Germany, had been arrested and deported. Seeking revenge for the suffering of his family. Grynszpan, who was 17 years old, bought a gun, went to the German embassy, and shot Vom Rath.

By 1939 Jews had been completely eliminated from the economic, cultural, and governmental life of Germany and Austria.

Herschel Grynszpan

Beginning in 1939, the passports of all Jews were marked with the letter "J". Also, the name Israel was added to the names of all Jewish males, and Sarah to all Jewish females.

Kristallnacht was an anti-Jewish pogrom on November 9-10, 1938. Jewish property, businesses, and synagogues were attacked and burned by Nazi mobs.

The Voyage of the Doomed

In a speech delivered on January 30, 1939, Adolf Hitler declared, "If a World War breaks out, the Jewish race in Europe will be eliminated." Thousands of frightened Jews fled from Germany to seek refuge in other countries. Thousands more would have done so but could not, because it was difficult to find a country that would allow them in.

Outside Germany, few people cared about what was happening there, and many felt that Hitler and his Nazis were a temporary phenomenon that would disappear. An anti-German boycott was organized in a few places, but it had little effect.

The countries of Europe and the Americas admitted only a small number of Jews. The immigration process was often controlled by anti-Semitic officials. Some officials would only cooperate if given a bribe.

The voyage of the *St. Louis* illustrates the indifference of the Western nations.

The St. Louis

On May 13, 1939, the passenger ship *St. Louis* left Hamburg with 930 German Jewish refugees aboard, all carrying landing certificates for Cuba. When the ship arrived in Havana, the Cuban government would not allow them to land. For nine days the *St. Louis* circled off Havana and Florida. On June 5, Cuba said the refugees could go ashore if they posted a $500,000 bond within 24 hours, but it was impossible to accumulate so large a sum in so short a time.

The United States, too, refused to admit the passengers. On June 6, the ship headed back to Europe. On June 11, the captain threatened to beach it on the English coast in order to delay its return to Germany. The British allowed 280 "enemy aliens" to enter.

On June 17, the *St. Louis* docked in the Belgian port of Antwerp and the Jews were allowed to land. Within 12 months the German blitzkrieg had overrun Europe and they were sent to the concentration camps where they ultimately were murdered.

Not just the passengers on the *St. Louis* but millions of Jews could have been saved from the Nazis, but the U.S. State Department chose to ignore the signs of their impending doom.

Shipload of Jews pleading for entrance to any country that would accept them.

Where Did the German Jews Go?

Some Jews were able to escape from Nazi Germany. Among the refugees were prominent bankers and merchants, writers and scientists.

Some went to European countries, others to the United States, where the first German Jews had settled in the mid-19th century. Many German Jews who had formerly ignored or opposed Zionism now emigrated to Palestine.

The Fourth Aliyah / 1924–1928

The Fourth Aliyah was of a different social background: It brought shopkeepers and artisans, mostly from Poland, where economic restrictions were being applied. The majority of the new arrivals settled in the cities of Tel Aviv, Haifa, and Jerusalem.

During the years 1924 to 1929, some 50,000 Jews came on aliyah to Israel. At the end of this period, the Jewish population of Israel was about 170,000.

The Fifth Aliyah / 1929–1939

The Land of Israel beckoned as a refuge. Although German Jews had often been ambivalent about Zionism, many of them now turned to the land of their ancestors. As a result the Fifth Aliyah, which extended from 1929 to 1939, was made up mostly of settlers from Germany and adjoining areas. The olim included students expelled from school by the Nazis, musicians, actors, artists, and writers whose work had been condemned as decadent, professionals unable to find work because of anti-Semitic restrictions, and manufacturers and businessmen no longer permitted to function in Germany. The skills, experience, and capital they brought had a major impact on the development of the Palestinian economy.

The Hebrew University was founded on Mount Scopus in Jerusalem in 1925. The first books for the library were brought on a donkey.

Many German Jews, however, hesitated to leave their homeland, the land where their ancestors had lived for hundreds of years. Like many other Germans, they still believed that Hitler's regime would soon come to an end.

June 7, 1936 edition of the *Palestine Post* detailing the beginning of the widespread terror and destruction which Arab uprisings were to inflict upon Jewish settlements during the next three years.

Henrietta Szold

One of the most important American Zionist activists was Henrietta Szold (1860–1945). In 1912, she founded Hadassah, an organization of American Zionist women. Over the years since, Hadassah has devoted itself to establishing hospitals and health and welfare services in Israel. These are open to everyone in the country, Jews, Arabs, Muslims, and Christians alike. The Hadassah Hospital and Medical Center in Jerusalem is widely regarded as the finest and most up-to-date medical facility in the entire Middle East.

Youth Aliyah

During the years preceding World War II, Henrietta Szold also organized Youth Aliyah to rescue as many children and adolescents as possible from Nazi Germany. Once the youngsters arrived in Palestine, Youth Aliyah placed them in homes and helped them to obtain schooling and vocational training. All this was done with the help of funds raised in America and other free countries. Youth Aliyah saved thousands of children. Their parents, naturally enough, found it difficult to part with them. Many fathers and mothers did not succeed in leaving Germany, but they were glad that at least their children would be safe.

The Growth of the Yishuv

The Jewish community of Palestine in the years before the State of Israel was founded was known as the Yishuv. Throughout the 1920s and 1930s it steadily grew larger and more diversified.

New industrial centers and kibbutzim were founded. Tel Aviv, founded in 1909 as a garden suburb of Jaffa, became a beautiful modern city. Stockade-and tower settlements, designed with an eye to defense against Arab marauders, sprang up throughout the land, especially in the undeveloped Negev area.

The Hebrew University

On the outskirts of the Old City of Jerusalem, in the area where Moses Montefiore had once built model houses, a new Jerusalem was coming into existence. In 1925 the Hebrew University was founded on Mount Scopus. Its first lecture was given by the great physicist Albert Einstein (1879–1955), and its first chancellor was Judah Magnes (1877–1948), a prominent American Reform rabbi. Under his leadership, scientists, scholars, and educators from all over the world now pursued their work in Jerusalem.

Today the Hebrew University has two main campuses, the original one on Mount Scopus and a new one at Givat Ram. Its facilities include medical and professional schools, an agricultural institute, and Israel's National and University Library, with over 2 million books.

Henrietta Szold (1860-1945), humanitarian and Zionist leader. After a distinguished career as educator and editor, she founded Hadassah and settled in Jerusalem, where she supervised Hadassah's social services and headed Youth Aliyah.

The Arab Situation

The progress the Jewish settlers were making was viewed with great anxiety by rich Arab landowners and many Muslim leaders. Arab propagandists stirred up hatred against the Jews, and anti-Jewish riots broke out repeatedly.

In 1936 the Grand Mufti of Jerusalem, religious head of Palestine's Muslim populace, helped to stir up a major Arab revolt. When the British tried to arrest him, he escaped to Lebanon and then to Germany. There he publicly endorsed Hitler's anti-Jewish program and spent the World War II years broadcasting Nazi propaganda to Muslims around the world.

As Jewish immigration increased, due to persecution in Europe, and Arab hostility intensified, the situation in Palestine became more and more difficult. In 1939 a British commission of inquiry proposed that the country should be divided into two parts, one Jewish, the other Arab. The Arabs rejected the proposed partition and stepped up their anti-Jewish activities. But the Yishuv kept right on growing.

was from Germany, Austria, and Czechoslovakia. As the Nazi terror spread, Jews came to Palestine from Poland, Rumania, Bulgaria, and Yugoslavia. A few even managed to leave Russia, despite the danger of being arrested or killed by Communist border guards.

The people of the Yishuv learned to live together and to know one other. To a great extent this was made possible by the fact that they had a common language—Hebrew. The language of the Bible had been transformed into a modern tongue. It was used by poets and writers, scientists, farmers and workers, cab drivers, and housewives doing their shopping. Newspapers were published in Hebrew, unions recruited members in Hebrew, and the Va'ad Leumi, the Yishuv's governing body, conducted its affairs in Hebrew.

In the land which had been the scene of biblical history, a new Jewish community was building a new life using the language of the Bible in everyday speech for the first time in 2,000 years.

New Immigrants

The population of the Yishuv was made up of Jews from many lands and many walks of life. It included Jews from Iraq, Yemen, and North Africa who were very similar in culture to their Arab neighbors. There were many from Eastern Europe, and a few from the United States. In the 1930s, with Hitler in power, most of the new immigration

A 1948 Histadrut poster issued after the War of Independence features the theme of physical labor and vigilance.

A stockade-and-tower settlement established during the 1930s. Despite British disapproval, the settlements were set up under cover of night. Walls provided protection against attacking Arabs.

The Evian Conference / 1938

In May 1938, officials of 32 nations met at Evian-les-Bains, in France, to find a way of dealing with the flow of refugees from Nazi Germany. The United States was represented by Myron C. Taylor, former chairman of the U.S. Steel Corporation. With the exception of the Netherlands and Denmark, every country made clear its unwillingness to accept significant numbers of refugees.

Australia, with vast, unpopulated areas, announced: "As we have no real racial problem, we are not desirous of importing one."

New Zealand refused to lift its immigration restrictions.

Britain declared that its colonial empire "contained no territory suitable to the large-scale settlement of Jewish refugees."

Canada only wanted immigrants with farming experience and would take no one else.

France, whose population already included 200,000 refugees and 3 million aliens, stressed that it had reached its saturation point.

Nicaragua, Honduras, Costa Rica, and Panama issued a joint statement that they could accept no "traders or intellectuals."

Argentina, with a population one-tenth that of the United States, reported that it had welcomed almost as many refugees as the United States and hence could not be counted on for large-scale immigration.

And the United States, the nation at whose initiative the conference had convened, what would it offer? The answer was soon forthcoming. The United States, with its tradition of asylum, its vast land mass, and its unlimited resources, agreed, for the first time, to accept its full, legal quota of 27,370 immigrants annually from Germany and Austria—a totally inadequate figure in light of the huge number of Jews desperately seeking someplace to go. That was the major American concession made at Evian.

Some historians feel that the Evian Conference taught the Nazis that the world, for all its moralistic posturing, was unwilling to do much about the persecution of Jews in Germany. Noting that Evian spelled backwards is naive, they say that the Jewish delegates were naive to ever have expected help from the assembled nations.

FOREIGN-BORN POPULATION IN THE UNITED STATES IN 1920

GERMANY 1,683,298
ITALY 1,607,458
RUSSIA 1,398,999
POLAND 1,139,578
GREAT BRITAIN 1,133,967
CANADA 1,117,136
IRELAND 1,035,680
SWEDEN 624,759
AUSTRIA 574,959
MEXICO 476,676
HUNGARY 397,081
NORWAY 363,599
DENMARK 189,051
GREECE 175,701
FRANCE 152,792
FINLAND 149,671
HOLLAND 131,262
SWITZERLAND 118,647
ASIA 110,586
RUMANIA 103,007

Immigrant quotas for each country were fixed in such a way as to keep the proportion of foreign-born Americans the same as it was in 1920. In practice it proved superfluous, since in the thirties immigration dropped to an average of just over 10,000 a year.

The British White Paper / 1939

With the growth of the Yishuv, Arab resistance increased. The English, unwilling to antagonize the Arabs, could not deal with this friction between Arabs and Jews. The Jews secretly organized their own defense groups of men and women of the Yishuv, farmers and workers, city and country folk. These citizens trained to defend themselves against Arab terrorists who preyed upon isolated settlements. This group of defenders took the name of Haganah ("defense").

The White Paper

The British White Paper of 1939 declared that in 10 years Palestine would be partitioned, and in the meantime Jewish immigration would be severely restricted. This document was a complete and utter disavowal of the Balfour Declaration and of Great Britain's international obligations under the Mandate. The British appeasement of the Arabs was motivated by fear that the Arabs would support Germany, and threaten England's hold on the Middle East, if war broke out in Europe.

In 1939 the British government invited Iraq, Jordan, and Egypt, the Palestinian Arabs, the Jewish Agency, and Jews in Britain and America to send representatives to London to discuss the political future of Palestine. The Arabs refused to meet with the Jews, and two separate sets of meetings were held.

Prime Minister Neville Chamberlain presides over the Jewish representatives at the abortive London Conference of February 1939. Shortly after the conference the British government published its White Paper, freezing Jewish immigration to Palestine. The participants included Nahum Goldmann, Chaim Weizmann, David Ben-Gurion, and Moshe Sharett, each of whom became an important figure in the State of Israel.

The Desperate Search for Refuge

The publication of the White Paper of 1939 brought consternation to Jews everywhere. What would happen now to the Jews in the lands under Nazi domination? Where would they go? Restrictions on immigration were increasing in every country; even the gates of America were closing, for so many Jews had emigrated there that the German, Polish, Czech, and Austrian quotas were now filled.

The Jews of Europe went wherever they could. However, it became increasingly difficult to find a place of refuge. Some fled to South America, to Africa, and even to war-torn Shanghai. But even so, only a few could manage to escape at this late date. President Franklin D. Roosevelt had called an international conference at Evian-les-Bains, France, in 1938 to discuss ways and means of saving European Jewry. The conference was a dismal failure. The results of other endeavors were equally meager.

Secret message from a British spy warning of the activities of two "underground" ships, the *Colorado* and the *Atratti*. In 1939, these two ships, crammed with desperate Polish-Jewish refugees escaping Hitler's Holocaust, were intercepted by British warships and turned back. There is evidence that some of the spies were Jewish traitors who sold out to the British.

Aliyah Bet

In these dark days a desperate new kind of aliyah was started. Operating illegally and in secret, it was called Aliyah Bet—Immigration Wave B. Agents of the Haganah, the Yishuv's underground defense force, secretly began transporting refugees from Europe to Palestine. Some of their ships were intercepted by the British, but many others got through, Their human cargo would be landed on deserted beaches, late at night, and quickly spirited away to hiding places on the kibbutzim.

A boatload of "illegal" immigrants landing in Palestine under cover of darkness

The Western Democracies

The Western democracies feared another conflict on the scale of World War I and did everything possible to appease Hitler. His appetite for aggression was endless. After swallowing up Austria and Czechoslovakia without having to strike a blow, he attacked Poland in September 1939. The Poles fought back; Britain and France, aware that appeasement did not work, declared war on Germany.

The three leaders of the war against the Nazis with their advisors. *From left to right,* Winston Churchill of England, Franklin Delano Roosevelt of the United States, and Stalin of Russia.

The Second World War Begins

On April 9, 1940 the Germans attacked and overran Norway and Denmark. Soon after, Holland, Belgium, Luxembourg and France were attacked. None of the armies could withstand the fast-moving German armor and their deadly air strikes.

By June 22, France sued for peace and 330,000 British and French troops were evacuated from the beaches of Dunkirk to England.

Millions of Jews were now under German control. Hitler felt that he was now in a position to solve the "Jewish Question." As Hitler saw it, the Jewish Question was simply the fact that Jews existed. He and his criminal cohorts devised a "Final Solution" as a way to eliminate the Jews. In all countries under Nazi control, Jews were rounded up, confined to ghettos, or shipped to concentration camps.

The Blitzkrieg

At first, Hitler had everything his own way, and his armed forces was victorious on every front. By 1941 his troops had conquered most of Europe: Norway, Denmark, Holland, Belgium, France, Yugoslavia, and Greece. Britain stood alone and was hard-pressed, despite Lend-Lease aid from the United States. Then Hitler attacked the Soviet Union. His winning streak continued for a while, but by 1943, with both the Soviet Union and the United States allied against him, the tide finally turned.

The German commander's first announcement: "The German soldiers have come to free the population from Communist bondage. The Jews must wear armbands with a Star of David, they must not leave their quarters; they must carry out their required work and yield their radios."

The Master Race

The Final Solution

Germany's victories brought millions of Jews under Nazi control. The Final Solution was now put into effect to kill all of Europe's Jews. The details of the program were worked out by a group of Nazi officials at the Wannsee Conference in January 1942.

In every occupied country, Jews would be rounded up, confined to ghettos, then shipped to concentration camps. Most would be killed outright. Some would be used as slave laborers until they were too worn out, from starvation and harsh treatment, to be useful. Among the most notorious of the death camps were Chelmo, Sobibor, Treblinka, and Auschwitz. The treatment of the inmates was almost beyond rational description. By the end of the war, somewhere between 3 million and 4 million Jewish inmates had been gassed and their bodies incinerated. Overall about 6 million Jews were killed. Many thousands of non-Jews, opponents of the Nazis, were also killed in the camps.

After the war Eli Wiesel, Primo Levi, and other survivors wrote gripping accounts of their terrible experiences in the camps. In addition, the Nazis kept methodical records of what they were doing, and some of the more sadistic took photographs as "souvenirs."

SS Colonel Adolf Otto Eichmann was chief of operations in the scheme to exterminate all of European Jewry. At the end of the war, he escaped to Argentina, but in 1960 was kidnapped by the Israelis. Eichmann was tried before the Jerusalem District Court and was sentenced to death by hanging. Eichmann was the only criminal ever put to death in Israel. His body was cremated and his ashes were scattered over the Mediterranean.

BEFORE

Jewish men, women, and children being loaded onto cattle cars for shipment to the death camps.

AFTER

A heap of concentration camp victims.

Anne Frank

Growing up in Frankfurt, Germany, Anne Frank (1929–1945) dreamed about writing a novel and a book of poems. Sadly, Anne's dream was shattered by the rise of Nazism. In 1933, the Frank family fled to Amsterdam to escape the Nazi regime. When the Germans occupied Holland in 1940, the Franks once again found themselves under the thumb of Hitler.

Into Hiding

Two years later in 1942, the Germans began deporting Holland's Jews, supposedly to work in labor camps. The Frank family and four other people went into hiding in the attic of a building owned by Anne Frank's father. War and conflict bring out the best and the worst in people. The hidden Jews were kept alive by friendly Gentiles who put their own lives in danger to bring them food and other necessities. However, an act of betrayal resulted in their discovery by the German police. All eight people in the attic were caught and sent to Bergen-Belsen, where Anne and six of the others died; only her father survived.

The Diary

During her time in hiding, Anne retained her equilibrium by writing short stories, beginning a novel, and keeping a diary. Anne's diary describes the constant fear of being discovered, the petty irritations and discomforts of being confined and living at close quarters with others, and the hopes and dreams of an adolescent filled with the spirit of life. In her diary she wrote, "I hear the approaching thunder which will destroy us. I can feel the sufferings of millions, and yet, if I look into the heavens, I think that it will all come right and that this cruelty will end, and peace and tranquility will return."

After the war, Anne's diary was discovered and published. It received instant acclaim and has been translated into many languages, dramatized on Broadway, and made into a film. The house in Amsterdam where the Frank family hid is now a museum.

Anne Frank's voice became the voice of six million vanished Jewish souls.

Anne Frank, the author of the "single most compelling personal account of the Holocaust"

The Anne Frank house in Amsterdam is now a museum.

The Dutch Church cooperated and issued baptismal certificates to Jews. Many Jews were saved because of these certificates.

Auschwitz

Auschwitz, the largest extermination complex, was located at a railroad junction in southern Poland. It consisted of three camps.

Auschwitz I was a labor camp and administration center. Within this camp were armament plants belonging to Siemens and Krupp.

Auschwitz II had a special extermination area called Birkenau where at least 1 million Jews were murdered. Its four gas chambers, using Zyklon-B, exterminated over 12,000 victims each day.

Auschwitz III had a huge I. G. Farben plant in which Jewish slaves labored to manufacture synthetic rubber from coal. The life expectancy of a Jewish worker in the rubber plant was three months; those in the coal mines that supplied the plant lasted 30 days.

The process of mass extermination was carried out with the full knowledge and cooperation of many business executives. They benefited by taking over Jewish-run

The Nazi death camp of Auschwitz. Thousands of Jews were gassed, shot, and burned to death there.

factories and businesses. They also benefited from the labor of the slaves who worked in their factories. I. G. Farben also earned a handsome profit by manufacturing Zyklon-B, the gas used in the extermination chambers.

Josef Mengele was physician of the Auschwitz camp, where he conducted cruel medical experiments on Jewish inmates. After the war, Mengele was traced to Argentina, but he escaped. These are some of Mengele's victims.

Concentration camp photo.

274

Gas Chambers and Ovens

Camps like Auschwitz, with their mass-production death machinery, were a product of German efficiency. Originally the Nazis had begun killing Jews by means of starvation and firing squads. By the winter of 1941, 1.5 million Jews had been eliminated, but the killing methods were too slow and inefficient. After a number of experiments, the system used at Auschwitz was devised.

Lined up at the railway station for shipment to a concentration camp.

The victims were assembled and packed in special sealed trains. On arriving in the camps they were forced into undressing rooms where they were shaved by barbers and stripped of their possessions. They were then packed into chambers and gassed. This highly efficient killing process could kill 2,000 Jews in the space of five minutes.

The Nazis mobilized Jewish slaves called Sonderkommandos to "process" the bodies. They removed gold fillings from teeth, shaved off the hair, then piled the bodies into crematoria where they were burned. In the meantime the clothing, hair, and other possessions were packed and sent to Germany for use in the war effort. Even the ashes of the victims were used— as fertilizer for German farms.

To minimize the possibility of a revolt in the camp, the Sonderkommandos were periodically exterminated and replaced with fresh slaves. Many of them, driven mad by their macabre duties and the fate of their fellow Jews, willingly joined the victims in the gas chambers rather than continue to do the bidding of the Nazis.

A German indoctrinating new troops on the fastest way to murder a Jew. Note his handiwork at the bottom of the pit.

Sonderkommandos at an extermination camp rushing to perform their duties. They too ended up in gas chambers and in mass graves.

American Jews Speak Up

In September 1941 the Germans began deporting Jews from elsewhere in Europe to concentration camps in Poland. The World Jewish Congress brought this to the attention of the Allied authorities in London and Washington.

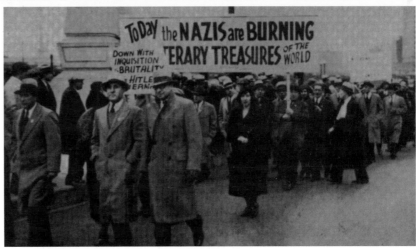

Anti-Nazi demonstration in New York City on May 10, 1933.

The Morgenthau Diaries

In his diaries, Secretary of the Treasury Henry Morgenthau Jr. (1891–1967), a Jewish member of President Roosevelt's cabinet, accused State Department officials of suppressing information about the atrocities.

According to some historians, hundreds of thousands of Jewish lives could have been saved if the White House and the State Department had not sabotaged efforts on their behalf. It has been suggested that President Roosevelt was aware of the deportations but deliberately refused to interfere.

The Morgenthau diaries record, "On December 17, 1943, the State Department received a cable from London. . . . the British Foreign Office was concerned with the difficulty of resettling considerable numbers of Jews should they be released. For this reason we are reluctant to approve financial arrangements. The financial arrangements would have permitted the World Jewish Congress to spend 100 million Rumanian leis for the release of thousands of Jewish children in France and Rumania."

While the politicians debated, millions of Jews were being gassed and incinerated into piles of ashes.

The Extermination Plot

On August 8, 1942 Gerhard Regner, the representative of the World Jewish Congress in Geneva, sent a telegram to the State Department detailing the mass murder of Jews taking place in Nazi-occupied Europe. The information came from the Allied underground, German deserters, and a report by SS Officer Kurt Gerstein, who had served in three extermination camps.

Sumner Welles, the Deputy Secretary of State, did not disclose the contents of the telegram to President Roosevelt. By the winter of 1942, information of Nazi atrocities had become public knowledge and the Allies could no longer ignore the facts. On December 17, 1942 they issued a statement condemning the mass exterminations.

Pope Pius XII, the head of the Roman Catholic Church, refused even to condemn the atrocities, explaining that the reports were exaggerated for propaganda purposes. To this day, the Vatican has not fully explained or dealt with the pope's failure to take action.

Why Auschwitz Was Not Bombed

Although the Allies knew about Auschwitz, they made no attempt to interfere with the killings. The Jewish Agency pressed the Allies to bomb the gas chambers and the railroad tracks leading to the camp. All such requests were turned down with the excuse that the operation would endanger the lives of the pilots and had no clear military purpose.

British Prime Minister Winston Churchill, who advocated the bombing, wrote to Anthony Eden, his Foreign Secretary, "There is no doubt that this is the most horrible crime ever committed in the history of the world."

The Allies certainly had the capability of bombing Auschwitz. This was demonstrated in August of 1944, when American aircraft attacked the synthetic rubber plant there. In addition, American planes based in Italy regularly bombed synthetic oil factories less than 5 miles from the gas chambers.

Why the Allies failed to bomb Auschwitz has never been fully explained. Had they done so, it is possible that many lives might have been saved.

The Brand Mission

In 1944 Adolf Eichmann, the Nazi official in charge of exterminating the Jews of Hungary, approached Joel Brand, a member of the Hungarian Zionist underground, and offered a deal. The German government would trade 100,000 Hungarian Jews for 10,000 trucks. Eichmann promised that the trucks would be used only on the eastern front against the Russians. Brand passed on this strange offer, but nothing came of it because the trucks would have helped the German war effort, and there was no way of knowing whether Eichmann could be trusted.

Meanwhile, on July 2, 1944, Allied planes bombed Budapest, the capital of Hungary. On July 7, fearing further raids, Admiral Horthy, the dictator of Hungary, halted all deportations of Jews. In the preceding three months, over 450,000 had been murdered.

On September 13, 1944, American airplanes bombed the industrial complex near Auschwitz. Several bombs were dropped by mistake on the camp itself, killing 15 SS men and scores of prisoners and workers.

The Warsaw Ghetto

The Judenrat

When the Germans captured Warsaw in 1939, there were 400,000 Jews living there. The Nazis confined them to a ghetto about 1 mile square and set up a Judenrat, headed by Adam Czerniakow (1880–1942), to govern the ghetto and carry out their orders.

Dr. Janusz Korczak, a physician, writer and educator, headed a children's orphanage in the Warsaw Ghetto. On August 12, 1942, he accompanied the children to the gas chambers, although he himself did not have to go.

The Judenrat members faced many very difficult moral decisions. They wanted to be able to help their fellow Jews but often had to do terrible things, such as selecting people for deportation. By forcing the Judenrat members to do this, and thereby making them unwilling accomplices to the Final Solution, the Nazis were purposely trying to degrade them. While the existence of the Judenrat seemed to give the Jews some control over their destiny, in reality it had no power to do anything except enforce Nazi orders. Refusal to carry out orders resulted in severe punishment.

Fifty Jewish combat groups—a thousand men and women armed with 80 rifles, three light machine guns, a few hundred revolvers, and 1,000 hand grenades—put up a desperate fight against 2,000 members of the occupying forces under SS General Stroop, who had been ordered to destroy the Warsaw Ghetto.

To the extent possible, the Judenrat tried to alleviate conditions in the ghetto. It maintained order and established hospitals, kitchens, schools, and recreation facilities. Clandestine religious services were also held, as were lectures and musical recitations. The ghetto residents also put out underground publications in Yiddish, Hebrew, and Polish with information on German activities and how to sabotage factories. In 1942, deportations to Treblinka began on a mass scale. Three days later Adam Czerniakow committed suicide rather than cooperate with the deportations.

The Ghetto Uprising

In the next few months the great majority of the ghetto's residents were deported and killed. On April 18, 1943 the underground learned that the Germans intended to wipe out the 50,000 remaining Jews. Everyone took shelter in carefully designed bunkers, and the 1,000 members of the ghetto's fighting organization, armed with homemade bombs and a few guns, prepared for the hopeless battle. Every man, woman, and child in the ghetto became a warrior.

On Passover morning, April 19, 1943, a heavily armed SS brigade moved into the ghetto. The surprised Nazi troops came under fire and suffered many losses in dead and wounded. To avoid street fighting, the Germans used artillery and flamethrowers.

It took four weeks of heavy fighting to obliterate the ghetto. When all the buildings were destroyed, the SS moved in with poison gas to kill the Jews who remained alive in hidden bunkers. A few survivors escaped through the sewers to other parts of Warsaw.

The Yishuv Fights

The Jewish Brigade

During World War II the men and women of the Yishuv gave valiant aid to Britain in the fight against Nazi tyranny. At the outset, David Ben-Gurion, the head of the Jewish Agency, spoke for all the Jews of Palestine: "We will fight the war as if there were no White Paper," he said, "and we will fight the White Paper as if there were no war."

Very few Palestinian Arabs fought in the war, but many Jewish settlers volunteered to serve in the British Army. The Nazis, anxious for a foothold in the Middle East, flooded the area with agents and propaganda. They found many sympathizers among extreme Arab nationalists who hated the British and opposed Jewish immigration to Palestine.

Eventually, the British permitted the Palestinian Jewish soldiers to organize their own Jewish Brigade and fight under their own blue-and-white flag, emblazoned with the Star of David.

Behind Enemy Lines

Volunteers from the Haganah carried out dangerous assignments behind enemy lines. Several were dropped by parachute into Nazi-occupied territory to make contact with the local resistance movements.

The Jewish fighters from Palestine who were parachuted behind enemy lines were part of the British intelligence service. They performed many missions for the Allies, as well as special missions for the Jewish people. Returning to their native lands using false names and false passports, they tried to organize ways to help Jews escape from the Nazi death camps. Many of them were captured and executed as spies.

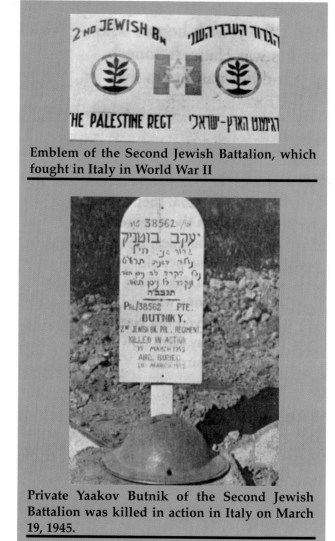

Emblem of the Second Jewish Battalion, which fought in Italy in World War II

Private Yaakov Butnik of the Second Jewish Battalion was killed in action in Italy on March 19, 1945.

Six volunteers who were about to parachute into occupied Europe to help their fellow Jews. Most of them were captured and executed by the Nazis.

Hannah Senesh

One of the Jewish heroes who operated in secret against the Nazis was Hannah Senesh (1921–1944). She had left her parents and a comfortable home in Budapest to live the life of a pioneer in Palestine. She was parachuted into Yugoslavia, where she contacted the resistance and aided their underground operations. After this mission was accomplished she made her way to Hungary to bring help to the Jews. There she was captured and put to death by the Nazis. Hannah Senesh had a strong, dedicated spirit. Before she died she wrote a poem, "Blessed Is the Match," in which she compared herself to a fiery match, which kindles a flame and is itself consumed in performing this task.

Enzo Sereni

Another hero was Enzo Sereni (1905–1944), an Italian Jew whose father had been a physician to the royal family of Italy. After going to Palestine as a pioneer, Sereni worked for the Haganah for years. While on a secret mission in German-occupied Italy, he was captured and killed.

Enzo Sereni (*second from right*), with Italian fellow officers, in 1926.

Hannah Senesh wrote this short letter before she parachuted into Yugoslavia.

The passport of Hannah Senesh

Leo Baeck—Hero of the Concentration Camps

There was another kind of heroism during this trying time—the quiet heroism displayed by Jews in the German concentration camps. Many of these martyrs preserved a spirit of hope and compassion despite bestial treatment by the Nazis.

Leo Baeck

Rabbi Leo Baeck (1873–1956), a brilliant preacher and a leader of liberal Judaism, was the spiritual leader of the Berlin Jewish community. When the Nazis came to power, Dr. Baeck, an old man of great courage and dignity, devoted himself entirely to the welfare of the Jewish community. He had many opportunities to leave Germany, but chose to remain there, ministering to his people and serving as head of the Reichsvertretung, the council which represented German Jewry before the Nazi government.

Theresienstadt

In 1943, Baeck was sent to the concentration camp of Theresienstadt. Despite the intolerable conditions, he conducted religious services, gave classes and lectures,

Rabbi Leo Baeck

and did everything possible to keep up the morale of his fellow inmates. The Nazis assigned the elderly Baeck the most degrading forms of physical labor but were unable to break his spirit.

Baeck survived the war and settled in London, where he became chairman of the World Union for Progressive Judaism.

Jews loaded onto trucks and on their way to the extermination chambers.

Joop Westerweel, a non-Jewish school principal in Holland, helped Jewish children escape over the Pyrenees into Spain. He was caught and executed by the Gestapo.

Righteous Gentiles

Thousands of heroic men and women who were not Jewish put themselves in mortal danger to save the lives of Jews fleeing the Nazi Holocaust. Some saved just one person or one family, others were able to help thousands. Whatever the number of their beneficiaries, these courageous people—the Righteous Among the Nations—did what they did because they believed it was right. Some of them were pious Christians who believed in a religion of love; others were simply decent human beings who rose above the horror. The files of the Yad Vashem Memorial in Israel are filled with their stories. Many of these heroes have been publicly honored in the years since the war.

Raoul Wallenberg

One of the most outstanding Righteous Gentiles was Raoul Wallenberg (1912–1947?), First Secretary of the Swedish embassy in Budapest.

The moment he arrived in Budapest, Wallenberg applied to the Hungarian government for a quantity of *Schutzbriefen*, safe-conduct passes stipulating that the bearer was protected by the Swedish embassy. The Hungarians agreed to give him 1,500, but he obtained an increase to 15,000 by bribing the officials.

In November of 1944, the Nazis began rounding up the Jews of Hungary and sending them to the death camps. Wallenberg boarded the trains and distributed safe-conduct passes to the outstretched hands, then told everyone with a pass to walk over to a caravan of cars marked with the Swedish colors. Repeatedly confronting the Nazis this way, Wallenberg saved thousands of Jewish lives.

After the Russians captured Budapest, they arrested Wallenberg, and he was never heard from again. According to some reports, he died in a Soviet prison camp.

Raoul Wallenberg

Raoul Wallenberg distributed Swedish passes like this one, with which he is believed to have saved at least 30,000 Jews.

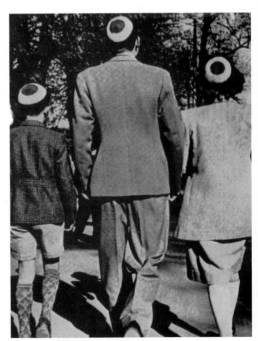

The Danes hit upon the idea of wearing skullcaps as a symbol of resistance and a token of unity with the Jewish people.

Holocaust Punishment

The death of Hitler and the German surrender (May 8, 1945) arrived too late for 12 million human beings, 6 million of whom were Jews. One-third of the entire Jewish people had been destroyed; barely 30 percent of the Jews of Europe remained alive.

The International Military Tribunal

Of the thousands who had perpetrated war crimes and the Holocaust, only a small fraction were brought to justice. In 1945, an International Military Tribunal was set up to prosecute Nazi war criminals. Meeting in Nuremberg, the tribunal tried a number of Nazi leaders: 12 were sentenced to death, and 3 were given life imprisonment. Hitler and Himmler had committed suicide just before the war ended, and Goering, who was sentenced to death by the tribunal, cheated the hangman by taking poison.

A session of the International Military Tribunal, Nuremberg, 1945–1946. In the dock are: (1) Hermann Goering, (2) Rudolf Hess, (3) Joachim von Ribbentrop, (4) Wilhelm Keitel, (5) Ernst Kaltenbrunner, (6) Alfred Rosenberg, (7) Hans Frank (8), Wilhelm Frick, (9) Julius Streicher, (10) Walther Funk, (11) Hjalmar Schacht, (12) Karl Doenitz, (13) Erich Raeder, (14) Baldur von Schirach, (15) Fritz Sauckel, (16) Alfred Jodl (17), Franz von Papen, (18) Arthur Seyss-Inquart, (19) Albert Speer, (20) Konstantine von Neurath, (21) Hans Fritzsche.

A few dozen minor war criminals were also tried by the Allies or by the Russians, but most were never caught or brought to trial, and an uncertain number escaped from Germany to South America or the Middle East, or even to the United States. Some former war criminals were protected by the American government, either working for the CIA in the Cold War struggle against Communism or, like Dr. Werner von Braun, helping to develop the space program.

Switzerland and the Holocaust

Switzerland was "neutral" during World War II. Many Jews anticipating problems, deposited their assets in Swiss banks. High-ranking Nazis also hid jewels, cash and gold, which they stole from their Jewish victims in numbered bank accounts.

Until 1997, the Swiss officially denied the existence of these Jewish and Nazi assets. However, under pressure of the World Jewish Congress, the Swiss have reluctantly opened their accounts and have agreed to return hundreds of millions of deposited and looted Jewish assets to Holocaust survivors.

The WJC also has documentary evidence regarding Nazi gold transfers and Jewish assets in other "neutral" countries such as Sweden, Turkey, Spain and Portugal.

As a consequence, the French government has appointed a committee to identify property stolen from French Jews. Over 2000 works of art in French museums have been identified as stolen from the Jews.

Foundations of the Holocaust

JEWISH HIGHLIGHTS

| The Beginning of Nazism 20th century | Looking for Refuge | Britain and Arabs | Searching for Refuge | Failure of the West |

JEWISH EVENTS • PERSONALITIES • LITERATURE • HOLIDAYS

The Beginning of Nazism 20th century
- Assassination of Walther Rathenau 1922
- Nazi Master Race
- Hitler comes to power / 1933
  Concentration camps
  Stormtroopers
  Nuremberg Laws
  Mein Kampf
- Kristellnacht
  Herschl Grynszpan
- Olympic Games
  Blacks and Jews

Looking for Refuge
- Fourth Aliyah / 1923
- Illegal aliyah
  St. Louis
- American Zionists
  Rabbi Abba Hillel Silver
  Felix Frankfurter
  Brandeis
- Henrietta Szold
  Hadassah
  Youth Aliyah

Britain and Arabs
- Grand Mufti
- Yishuv
  Stockade and Tower
  Settlements
  Vaad Leumi
- Hebrew language
- Evian Conference / 1938

Searching for Refuge
- British White Paper / 1939
- National Origins Act
- Immigration Quotas
- Aliyah Bet / 1939
  Underground Railroad

Failure of the West
- Surrender at Munich 1938
  Nevile Chamberlain
  Daladier
- World War II / 1940
- France surrenders
- Final Solution
- Wannsee Conference 1941
- Death camps
- Anne Frank
- Auschwitz
- Gas Chambers

WORLD HISTORY

- Death of the Weimar Republic
- Italian Fascism
- Il Duce

- Palestine
- America

- Palestine
- England

- France
- Myron C. Taylor

- Germany
- France
- England

The Holocaust

JEWISH HIGHLIGHTS

American Jewish Response 1940–1943	Warsaw Ghetto 1943	The Yishuv Fights 1941–1945	Heroes of the Spirit	Holocaust Punishment 6 Million Jews Killed

JEWISH EVENTS • PERSONALITIES • LITERATURE

American Jewish Response 1940–1943	Warsaw Ghetto 1943	The Yishuv Fights 1941–1945	Heroes of the Spirit	Holocaust Punishment 6 Million Jews Killed
▷ Henry Morgenthau	▷ Judenrat Adam Czerniakow	▷ Jewish Brigade	▷ Leo Baeck	▷ Hitler commits Suicide
▷ State Department turns deaf ear	▷ Jewish combat groups	▷ Haganah	▷ Raoul Wallenberg *Shutzbrief*	▷ Nuremberg Trials Hermann Goering
▷ Extermination plot Gerhard Regner	▷ Nazis destroy Warsaw Ghetto	▷ Hannah Szenesh	▷ Joop Westerweel	▷ Goering commits suicide
▷ Sumner Wells	▷ Janusz Korczak	▷ Enzo Sereni		▷ War criminals recruited by American industry
▷ Pope Pius XII				
▷ Auschwitz deliberately not bombed				
World Jewish Congress				

WORLD HISTORY

American Jewish Response 1940–1943	Warsaw Ghetto 1943	The Yishuv Fights 1941–1945	Heroes of the Spirit	Holocaust Punishment 6 Million Jews Killed
▷ Vatican	▷ Poland	▷ Italy	▷ Holland	▷ International Military Tribunal Nuremberg
Poland		▷ Palestine	▷ Sweden	
Geneva				
I. G. Farben				
Dutch underground				

Displaced Persons

In the liberated concentration camps, there were hundreds of thousands of displaced persons (DPs), former prisoners or slave laborers who had nothing to return to and no place to go. The war and the Nazis had uprooted them and destroyed their lives.

The problem of the Jewish displaced persons was particularly acute. Most of the few Jews who had managed to survive no longer had homes or families. Many of them wanted to go to Palestine.

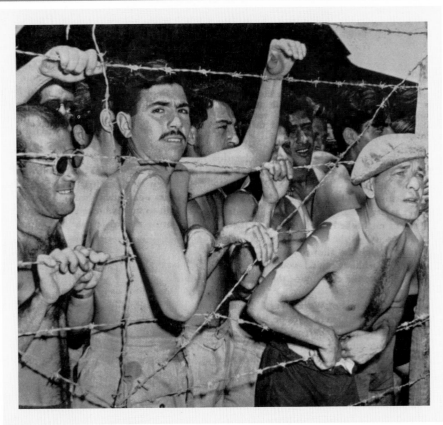

Refugees at a detention camp strain at the barbed wire that keeps them from freedom and their homeland.

Illegal Immigration

Unfortunately, the British White Paper of 1939 was still in effect, a pitiless barrier to further Jewish immigration to Palestine.

The Haganah, which had aided illegal immigration during the war in spite of the White Paper, again went into action. "Underground railroads" were again organized. The survivors of Hitler's death camps waiting in detention centers had cause for new hope.

Again, the Haganah took on the perilous task of landing illegal immigrants in secret, under cover of night. Often the passengers, young and old, many of them scarred by years of camp life, had to wade through a stormy surf or row in small boats to elude the British guards.

The Irgun Zvai Leumi, a Palestinian underground movement founded in 1937 by members of the Betar youth organization and the Zionist Revisionist movement, was also very active in the "illegal" immigration of Jewish displaced persons.

The Internment Camps

The British showed little sympathy for the plight of the Jews. Their main concern was to maintain good relations with the Arab nations and avoid trouble in the Middle East. They used their military forces to prevent Jewish immigration and succeeded in intercepting most of the ships. The passengers were arrested and sent to internment camps especially set up for them on the island of Cyprus. There, once again behind barbed wire and watched by armed guards, they awaited the moment when they would be able to ascend to the homeland.

The S.S. "Exodus"

In 1947 the British policy became even more harsh. In order to set an example, they sent back to Germany the S.S. *Exodus*, a Haganah boat crammed full of illegal immigrants, men, women and children who had survived the Nazi death camps. These refugees had risked their lives to come to Palestine. Now they were sent back to Germany, where there was no room for them except in DP (displaced persons) camps where, for all they knew, they might languish forever without home or hope.

The fate of the *Exodus* stirred the Jews of Palestine to open revolt. Haganah and Irgun units destroyed British radar stations, bridges, and other military installations, and attacked British patrols. Arms were manufactured in secret factories and smuggled in from abroad.

The Palestine Problem

As the situation deteriorated, the British closed-door policy became a matter of world concern. Britain being unable to solve the Palestine problem, the United Nations took up the question. In 1947 it sent a Committee of Inquiry to Palestine. The committee returned with a proposal to partition Palestine into two states—one Arab and one Jewish.

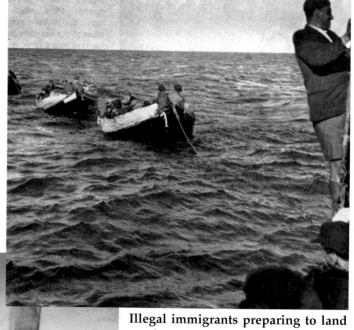

Illegal immigrants preparing to land on the coast of Palestine. The immigrants were transferred into small boats and under cover of darkness landed on the shores of the Promised Land.

The *Exodus*, a Haganah ship, carried 4,500 Jewish refugees to Palestine from the camps in Europe at the end of World War II. The British, still holding the mandate over Palestine, refused to allow the ship to dock and returned it to Hamburg, Germany. This brutal act helped swing world opinion against Britain and toward the creation of a Jewish state.

The Zionist Spokesmen

Before World War I, there were about 20,000 active Zionists in the United States. Most of them were affiliated with the Federation of American Zionists, which in 1917 was renamed the Zionist Organization of America. Associated with the ZOA were Hadassah, the women's Zionist organization; the Sons of Zion, a fraternal order; and Young Judaea, a youth group. There were also American branches of the Socialist Zionist Party (Poale Zion) and the Orthodox Mizrachi Party.

The ZOA and its affiliates was largest in size and put forth major spokesmen who fought for the formation of a Jewish state. The dynamic oratory of Louis Lipsky, Stephen S. Wise, and Abba Hillel Silver moved thousands of Jews at national Zionist conventions and helped persuade the general American public to support the Zionist cause.

By 1930 the number of active Zionists in the United States rose to 150,000. The growth of the Nazi movement in Europe aroused many American Jews. By 1940 there were 400,000 enrolled Zionists, and at the highest point, following World War II, there may have been twice that many.

America Speaks

In 1943 the American Jewish Conference made it clear that most American Jews favored statehood. During the United Nations deliberations on the partition of Palestine in 1947, American Jewry spoke out almost unanimously for this cause. The UN's decision to establish separate Jewish and Arab states in the mandated territory of Palestine was hailed with joy by American and world Jewry.

Rabbi Meir Berlin (*left*), American president of the Mizrachi World Organization, talking with Jewish Agency leader David Ben-Gurion

American public opinion, a series of resolutions passed by Congress, and the favorable attitude of President Truman all carried weight in persuading the nations of the world to vote for a Jewish state.

Poster of the American Zionist youth movement.

The State of Israel Is Born / 1948

Despite Arab protests, the United Nations passed a resolution in favor of partition on November 29, 1947. Jews everywhere rejoiced. Although the plan gave the Jews of the Yishuv only part of Palestine, the Jewish state of which generations had dreamed had become a reality. In Palestine Jews danced in the streets.

On May 14, 1948, the British gave up their mandate and left Palestine. The Jews at once set up a provisional government headed by David Ben-Gurion, and proclaimed the establishment of the State of Israel.

The emblem of Israel tells us a lot about the history and ideals of the Jewish people. The Temple menorah reminds us of the glory of the city of Jerusalem and also its sad destruction. The olive tree branches are symbols of peace. They tell the world that Israel wishes to live in peace with its neighbors.

War of Independence

The Arabs bitterly opposed the Partition Plan and refused to accept the United Nations vote. On May 15, 1948, the day the State of Israel came into existence, the armies of Lebanon, Syria, Saudi Arabia, Jordan, Iraq, and Egypt jointly attacked, vowing to drive the Jews into the sea. The British, before leaving the country, did all they could to help the Arab invaders. The Arabs had the advantage of superior numbers and weapons.

The Israelis fought valiantly, holding out against ferocious attacks by Arab artillery, armored cars, and aircraft. On isolated kibbutzim in the Galilee and the Negev, settlers defended themselves with rifles, mortars, and homemade Molotov cocktails. Although the Arabs appeared to have the upper hand when the war began, the tide soon turned. They were defeated on every front.

In January 1949, after months of fighting and thousands of casualties on both sides, a truce was declared. Twenty months after the first attack, the severely beaten Arab governments agreed to end the war.

Israel's stunning victory came at great human cost. More than 4,000 of its bravest soldiers and 3,000 civilians lost their lives defending the homeland.

The yearning of so many Jews, during the 2,000 years of exile, was now realized. Israel was reborn! The Jews now had a homeland of their own.

A banner headline announces the birth of the new state. Although the State of Israel was proclaimed on Friday afternoon, May 14, 1948, the paper is dated Sunday, May 16, because the *Palestine Post* in Israel was not printed on the Jewish Sabbath.

The Haganah

During the First and Second Aliyot, there were many Arab attacks against Jewish settlements in Eretz Yisrael. Hundreds of Jews were murdered and much property was destroyed. In response the Jews "rose up" and established Hashomer ("The Watchman"). This tiny defense force had only 100 members. But each of them was a deadly marksman, an expert horseman, and fluent in Arabic.

The Haganah Is Founded

In 1920, Hashomer was disbanded and a much larger defense force called Haganah ("The Defense") was established. Haganah members, both male and female, took responsibility for defending Jewish towns and settlements.

When Arab riots swept the country in 1929, Haganah volunteers saved the Jewish communities of Jerusalem, Tel Aviv, and Haifa from destruction. After 1929 Haganah began a period of expansion and improved training. Modern arms were smuggled into Palestine in barrels of cement and agricultural machinery crates. By 1939, the Haganah had 25,000 members armed with smuggled rifles, machine guns, and homemade grenades manufactured in secret factories.

After World War II, the British continued their pro-Arab policy of restricting Jewish immigration into Eretz Yisrael. The Haganah countered by destroying British radar stations, bridges, and other military establishments. Haganah's main activity during the period of 1945–1948 was the organization of illegal immigration into Palestine. Tens of thousands of so-called "illegal immigrants" were smuggled into the country.

On May 31, 1948 the Haganah officially became Tzahal, the regular army of Israel.

A Haganah member stands guard at a defense perimeter.

This photo was taken at Kibbutz Hanita in 1938. *Left to right:* Moshe Dayan, Yitzhak Sadeh, and Yigal Allon. Each of these young men became a high-ranking officer in the Haganah as well as an important political leader.

The First Years of the New State

In January 1949 an armistice was declared. The State of Israel held elections and formed its first government. Dr. Chaim Weizmann, the revered Zionist leader, became its first President and David Ben-Gurion its first Prime Minister. In May 1949, Israel was admitted to the United Nations.

To many who witnessed the birth of Israel it seemed like a miracle. After pain and hopelessness, after the deaths of 6 million martyred Jews, the day of liberation had dawned for the survivors.

The State of Israel had many problems. It was a small country, and most of the holy places of Jewish tradition were in Arab territory. Hebron, with the cave of Machpelah and the graves of the Patriarchs, was outside Israel. Even the Old City of Jerusalem, and the Western Wall area, where once the Temple stood, were not in Israeli territory.

Exodus and Absorption

To compound Israel's difficulties, the Arab states remained hostile after the armistice, so defense was a major concern. In addition, there were vast numbers of newcomers to be absorbed—DPs from Europe and from British internment camps, as well as hundreds of thousands of refugees from Arab countries where Jews were no longer welcome. All of them had to be provided with food, medical care, a place to sleep, classes in Hebrew; ultimately, they needed jobs and homes as well.

Israel was an energetic young country. Its cities and villages were growing. Jews from many walks of life, many cultures, and many different nations eagerly began learning to live together. Many of them were devoted to Orthodox traditions and teachings. Others had no religious affiliations but were dedicated to building and developing the homeland. The doors of the new land were open to any Jew who wished to come and live there.

Almost immediately after the establishment of the State of Israel a campaign was organized to rescue the Jews of Yemen, Iraq, and Iran from persecution. They were evacuated by plane and brought safely to Israel. This courageous project was known as Operation Magic Carpet.

IMMIGRATION (Aliyah) FROM ARAB COUNTRIES

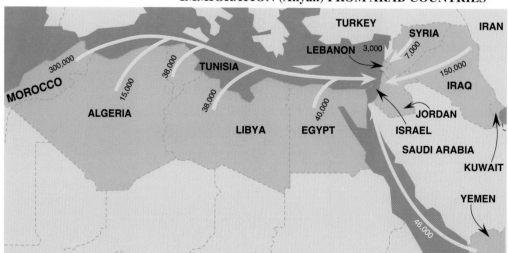

Israeli independence had a tremendous effect on Jewish communities in Arab lands. Most of the Arab countries instituted severe restrictions on their Jewish citizens. The hostile governments deprived them of their properties, their homes, and their businesses. These repressive measures initiated a huge exodus of Jews. Most of them arrived penniless, with only the clothes on their backs. In 1949, Operation Magic Carpet evacuated 50,000 Jews from Yemen.

The Suez Campaign / 1956

The War of Independence in 1948 was followed by a short period of quiet. For Israel it was the best of times; for eight years there was no large-scale shooting war. For Israel it was also the worst of times. For eight years there was a series of threats and terrorist attacks against the infant state.

In 1956, President Gamal Abdel Nasser of Egypt closed the Suez Canal to Israeli shipping and ships trading with Israel. The Arabs applied pressure against Israel on all sides, slowly choking its economy. Israel needed to keep its shipping lanes open, for they were its lifeline to the outside world, but diplomatic efforts failed to make the Egyptians relent.

On October 29, 1956, Israel attacked Egypt, operating in coordination with France and Britain, which hoped to regain control of the Suez Canal. In an eight-day campaign, the Israeli forces, under the command of General Moshe Dayan (1915–1981), captured the Gaza Strip and the entire Sinai Peninsula.

At this point the United States and the Soviet Union stepped in, forcing the British and French to withdraw from the Canal. Israel withdrew from Sinai, but only after a

Israeli soldiers shout in triumph as they reach the Suez Canal.

United Nations peacekeeping force was stationed along the Egypt-Israel border. As part of the settlement the United Nations guaranteed that Israeli shipping would have complete access to the Suez Canal.

Israel was now in a position to develop trading links with the Asian and African countries. It also now had an open port, Eilat, for importing oil from the Persian Gulf.

Israeli armored column waiting its turn to cross the Suez Canal.

Eichmann the Butcher

Jews have long memories, and sometimes many years pass before a wrong against them is avenged. After World War II many of the monsters who murdered Jews during the Holocaust escaped. Some found a safe haven in Arab countries. Many escaped to South America, where they lived under new identities. In many instances they were protected by anti-Semitic government officials.

Israel organized a special group of secret Nazi hunters whose job it was to find and expose these criminals.

In 1941, Adolf Eichmann had become head of the Department of Jewish Affairs at Nazi headquarters in Berlin. Eichmann organized the deportation of Jews to the death camps and was responsible for stealing their property. He had personally supervised the effort to destroy Hungarian Jewry.

After the war Eichmann was captured by the Allies, but in 1950 he managed to escape to Argentina. Friendly officials fur-

Eichmann on trial in Israel.

nished him with false identity papers, and he lived there till 1960, when he was discovered by the Israeli Nazi hunters. Eichmann was kidnapped and secretly flown to Israel. After a long trial he was found guilty and sentenced to death. His body was cremated, just as he had cremated 6 million Jews, and his ashes were scattered over the Mediterranean Sea.

His was the first and only execution ever carried out by the State of Israel.

The Yad Vashem Memorial: Ohel Yizkor - Hall of Remembrance. The walls are built of large, unhewn black lava rocks. On the mosaic floor are inscribed the names of the 21 largest concentration camps, and near the wall in the west burns a light.

The Six-Day War / 1967

June 1967 will be forever remembered as one of the most fateful periods in the history of Israel. For six fantastic days, the Middle East crossroads was torn by gunfire and screaming rockets. Then all was still. On the seventh day, when the smoke had cleared, the map of the world had been altered.

Israeli tanks blast their way up the Golan Heights in Syria.

The tension was terrific on Sunday, June 4. Tel Aviv and Cairo buzzed with rumors. Tiny Israel, hemmed in by foes, listened to bulletins coming over the radio station Kol Yisrael: Syria had joined Egypt and Jordan in a military alliance. President Nasser of Egypt had proclaimed that Israel would be driven into the sea. Ahmed Shukairy, head of the Palestine Liberation Organization, arriving in Amman, stated: "When we take Israel, the surviving Jews will be helped to return to their native lands." Then he added: "But I think that none will survive."

The cities of Israel were empty of men—those 18 to 49 had left for the army. Yet spirits were high in this country of 2.5 million people, the size of Massachusetts, all included in one telephone book. Surrounded by 110 million Arab enemies, Israelis dug foxholes and trenches and marked time. And there was evening and there was morning . . . Monday, June 5.

A decade had passed, during which the Arabs had plotted revenge. In the spring of 1967, bolstered by a huge supply of Russian armaments, Nasser felt the time had come for action. He forced the 3,400-man UN force to withdraw from its buffer position in the Sinai and then blockaded the Strait of Tiran, shutting off Israeli shipping from the East. This was an act of war.

Israel Strikes

On June 5, 1967 Israeli planes made a pre-emptive strike against Egyptian, Jordanian, and Syrian air bases. Swooping out of the skies, the Israelis destroyed 450 enemy planes. With lightning speed, Israeli armored columns smashed through the Egyptian army in the Sinai, not stopping until they reached the Suez Canal.

Before the war began, Israel had promised King Hussein of Jordan that no harm would come to his country if he stayed out of the fighting. Hussein ignored the peace overture and attacked Jerusalem. Israel counterattacked, and within a few days had defeated the Jordanians. Israeli forces were now in control of the West Bank (Judea and Samaria), and had captured the Old City of Jerusalem. The Temple Mount was under Jewish rule for the first time in almost 2,000 years.

Jerusalem Liberated / 1967

By Thursday, Egypt and Jordan had been defeated. The Old City of Jerusalem, liberated at great sacrifice by the unbelievable bravery of paratroops under Colonel "Motke" Gur, was in Jewish hands.

Hardened soldiers, who had wrestled with death in the fight to free the city, rushed to the Western Wall. There they found an outlet for their emotions. Some kissed the ancient stones. Others wept for friends who had fallen in Jerusalem's streets.

Soldiers cheered as they saw the blue-and-white flag raised above the wall. Then—a hush as the blast of a shofar pierced the air. Chief Chaplain Shlomo Goren, among the first to enter the Old City, had lifted the ram's horn to his lips for the historic call. Rabbi Goren offered a Yizkor prayer for the dead, and then somebody raised his voice in the Israeli national anthem, Hatikvah, and at once the sound swelled in a thousand throats.

Now, only Syria remained on the field of battle. The entire Israeli air force—some 400 planes—flew non-stop raids against deeply-dug Syrian gun emplacements on the heights above the Sea of Galilee. The morning sun on Shabbat revealed Syrians running toward Damascus on roads littered with equipment and clothing. Israel's ground forces then conducted a mopping-up operation. At 6:30 p.m. a ceasefire was put into effect. Thus, by June 10, after only six days, victorious Israeli troops had defeated the combined Arab armies. Israel had control of the entire Sinai Peninsula, the Golan Heights, the West Bank, and the Old City of Jerusalem. Meantime President Lyndon Johnson and Premier Alexei Kosygin, using the famous hot line, had assured each other that both superpowers wished only peace in the Middle East, and the UN Security Council had met in New York to hammer out a ceasefire resolution.

The capitals of the world breathed a sigh of relief. The tinderbox had not exploded. What might have spread into a global conflict had been confined, and the flames of war were snuffed out. The Israeli Chief of Staff, Major General Yitzhak Rabin (1922–1995) solemnly declared: "All this has been done by us alone, with what we have, without anybody else." Said Moshe Dayan: "We have returned to our holiest of places, never to depart again."

A few days later, on a sunlit day, these two great leaders joined Prime Minister Levi Eshkol (1895–1965) in a visit to the Kotel Ma'aravi (Western Wall), the last remnant of the Second Temple.

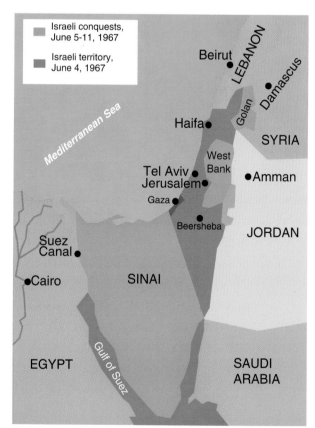

During the Six-Day War, Israel captured the Sinai, the Gaza Strip, the Golan Heights, and Judea and Samaria (West Bank).

Each one, following an old Jewish tradition, had written a prayer to place in a crevice in the wall. "What did you write?" curious reporters inquired. "Shema Yisrael," said Eshkol. "May peace be upon all Israel," said Dayan. "This is the Lord's doing; it is marvelous in our eyes," said Rabin, quoting Tehillim, the Book of Psalms.

A week after the war ended, on Shavuot, 200,000 Jews prayed at the Western Wall. Their tearful joy at the return of the sacred city expressed itself in prayer and in song.

The 28th of the month of Iyar, the day the city was liberated, is now celebrated in Israel as Jerusalem Day (Yom Yerushalayim). Israelis rejoice at the unification of the holy city, but sadly mourn the brave soldiers who fell in battle.

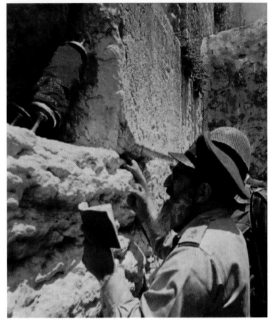

Rabbi Shlomo Goren, Chief Chaplain of the Israel Defense Forces, prays at the liberated Western Wall.

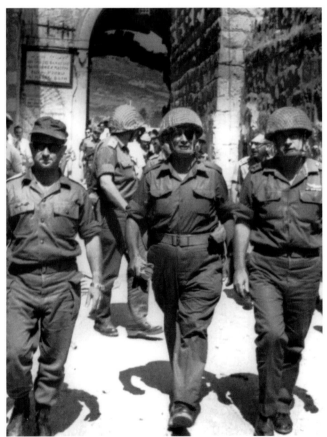

Entering the Old City of Jerusalem, *from left to right:* Chief of Staff Gen. Uzi Narkiss, Defense Minister Moshe Dayan, Gen. Yitzhak Rabin, commander of the Central Sector.

MOSHE DAYAN (1915–1981)
Israeli general and statesman: Moshe Dayan was born in Kibbutz Degania and at an early age was taken to live in Nahalal, the first moshav. As a teenager he joined the Haganah. During the Arab terrorist attacks in 1936, Dayan served in an elite commando force headed by Orde Wingate, a Bible-reading British officer who supported Zionism even though he was a Christian.

During Israel's War of Independence, Dayan held the rank of lieutenant colonel and commanded various fronts. He became a major general in 1953 and led the Israeli army during the Sinai Campaign in 1956.

In 1957 Dayan left the army to enter politics. Just before the Six-Day War in June 1967, Dayan was appointed Minister of Defense. After the great Israeli victory, Dayan administered the area occupied by the Israeli army on the West Bank of the Jordan River.

The Yom Kippur War / 1973

Almost daily between 1968 and 1973, marauding Arab terrorists sneaked across Israel's borders to attack innocent people. Tel Aviv was shelled. A school bus was blown up in Eilat injuring 28 children. Arab leaders encouraged their people to hate the Jewish state. Russia encouraged the Arabs and sent them billions of dollars worth of arms.

At the 1972 Olympics, Arabs murdered 11 Israeli athletes. In reprisal, Israel hit terrorist bases in Syria and Lebanon. Tensions in the Middle East rose steadily and ominously.

On October 6, 1973—the holy day of Yom Kippur—the Arabs attacked Israel on two fronts at once. Syria attacked Israel's northern Golan front, and Egypt attacked across the Suez Canal into the Sinai.

Since Yom Kippur is the most sacred day of the Jewish year, most soldiers were in the synagogues with their families. The Arab sneak attack succeeded and caught Israel off guard.

By the time Israel's troops could assemble to defend their land, the invading Arab armies had broken through the Israeli lines to both the north and the south. Massive Egyptian and Syrian armies penetrated Israel's defenses, the Egyptians pushing into Sinai and the Syrians moving into the Golan Heights.

By the third day, Israel recovered fast and started to take the offensive. With prayerbooks in one hand and machine guns in the other, Israeli soldiers left the synagogues and went straight to the battlefield. In nine days the Israeli army pushed back all the

An Arab poster depicts Israel as a snake. An Arab knife is severing its head from its body.

invaders. The Egyptian army was surrounded in the Sinai and Israeli troops threatened Cairo, Egypt's capital. The Syrians were also forced back, and Israel was poised to attack Damascus, Syria's capital.

Once it had become clear that Israel was winning, the Egyptians urged their Soviet backers to force an end to the fighting.

Russia and America Act

Meanwhile, a dangerous confrontation was brewing between the United States and Russia. The Soviet Union had been resupplying the Arabs. The losses suffered by the Israelis made resupply by America a vital necessity. At first the United States hesitated, but when it learned that the Russians were resupplying Egypt and Syria by means of the largest airlift in history, American planes began flying tons of equipment to Israel.

The Israeli participants in the 1972 Summer Olympics in Munich, Germany, prepare to board an El Al flight home, taking with them the bodies of 11 comrades who were brutally massacred by Arab terrorists.

Kissinger's Shuttle Diplomacy

Henry Kissinger (b. 1923) had come to America as a refugee from Hitler's Germany while still a boy. As Secretary of State in the administration of President Richard Nixon, he reasoned that the war was ending in a draw: the Arabs had fought well enough to recover their "honor," but now knew that even with the advantages of more manpower, better equipment, and complete surprise, they could not defeat Israel. In the agreement that Kissinger worked out with the Russians, Israel was to refrain from completely destroying the Arab armies, and direct talks were to begin between Israel and Egypt aimed at a "just and durable peace" in the region.

The Ceasefire

By the time the ceasefire took effect, Israel had managed to trap over 20,000 men, Egypt's elite Third Army. An Egyptian defeat on such a scale was unacceptable to the Russian patrons of the Arabs, and would also have upset the battlefield stalemate Kissinger wanted in order to force the start of peace negotiations.

On October 24 the Russians sent President Nixon a message in which they threatened to take matters into their own hands if America did not force Israel to withdraw from its advanced positions west of Suez, thereby freeing the trapped Third Army. The United States could not allow Russia to intervene directly in the Middle East. Nixon ordered American nuclear forces around the globe to be put on alert. For a few hours a much more destructive type of war seemed to menace the world, but a compromise was reached. Instead of Russian or American troops, a neutral UN force was sent to patrol the ceasefire lines. Israel allowed food and water to reach the Third Army but kept it trapped.

More than 11,000 Arabs died in the Yom Kippur War, but so did over 2,500 Israelis. Israel emerged victorious on the battlefield, but at a bloody price.

After the ceasefire, all Israel mourned the nation's loss of its soldiers. Prime Minister Golda Meir (1898–1979) said: "For the people of Israel, each human life is precious. Our dead soldiers are the sons of all of us. The pain we feel is felt by all of us."

As a result of the surprise attack, Golda Meir was forced to resign. Many voters had lost confidence in her. Yitzhak Rabin, of the Labor Party, became the new Prime Minister.

Secretary of State Henry Kissinger *(right)* **talks to Abba Eban** *(left)* **and Yigal Allon** *(center)* **during his shuttle diplomacy which led to a settlement between Israel and Egypt in 1979.**

Golda Meir / *1898–1979*

Women played an important role in the creation of the State of Israel. They were members of the First Aliyah and of every other wave of settlers. Young and old women were in the thick of the fighting during each of Israel's wars.

Golda Meir

Golda Meir was one of Israel's outstanding heroines. She was born in Kiev, Russia, where her father was a carpenter. There Golda Meir witnessed the violent pogroms against the Jews. Later in life she said that her childhood memories of the pogroms influenced her to become a Zionist.

When Golda was eight years old, her family moved to the United States and settled in Milwaukee, where she became a schoolteacher. In 1921 she and her husband, Morris Meyerson, moved to Palestine, where they joined a kibbutz. As a symbol of their dedication to the Jewish homeland, they changed their name from Meyerson to Meir, which means "giver of light."

Golda Meir became active in politics and was elected to head the Histadrut, Israel's central labor union. In 1948, before the War of Independence, she disguised herself as an Arab and secretly visited Emir Abdullah of Jordan in an effort to persuade him to keep his country out of the war. In 1949 Golda Meir became a member of the Knesset and Minister of Labor. She also served as Israel's first ambassador to the Soviet Union.

Golda Meir's organizational abilities propelled her onto the international political stage, first as Foreign Minister and in 1969 as the first female Prime Minister of Israel. After serving as Israel's leader during the Yom Kippur War, she submitted her resignation. In 1974, because of ill health, she retired from all of her political posts. When she died on December 8, 1978, people all over the world mourned this great and courageous woman.

President and Mrs. Richard Nixon of the United States with Prime Minister Golda Meir of Israel at the White House in 1972.

Rescue at Entebbe / 1976

Wars are fought on many different levels. There are battlefields where soldiers, tanks, and airplanes shoot at each other. But there is also war by terrorism directed against innocent civilians. Bombs are planted in department stores, civilians are shot or stabbed on the street, explosives are planted in automobiles.

On June 27, 1976 an Air France plane carrying 300 people was hijacked by terrorists. The plane, with its 300 passengers, was forced to land at Entebbe, the capital of the African nation of Uganda. The hijackers demanded that Israel release terrorists serving time in Israeli prisons in exchange for the passengers. This hijacking took place with the cooperation of the Ugandan government, headed by Idi Amin. He was known as the butcher of Uganda because of his savage cruelty. All non-Jewish prisoners were released, but more than 100 Jews were kept and threatened with death.

The Israel Defense Forces set up a plan called Operation Yonatan, named for its leader, Col. Yonatan (Yoni) Netanyahu. At a very young age Yoni Netanyahu had distinguished himself as an officer with the

Lieutenant Colonel Yonatan Netanyahu.

paratroopers. In 1967 he fought in the Six-Day War and was wounded. In 1973 he fought bravely in the Yom Kippur War. Now Yoni was entrusted with the job of freeing the Jewish prisoners in Entebbe.

Under cover of darkness, transport planes carried 100 highly trained Israeli commandos to Entebbe, more than 2,500 miles from Israel. The unmarked planes flew an indirect course to avoid detection.

The Israeli troops silently deplaned and in a short fight quickly eliminated the Ugandan troops and the terrorists. Within 90 minutes the hostages were on the plane and on the way back to safety.

There was one tragic death. Col. Yoni Netanyahu, the leader of the raiding party, was killed. His death was mourned by Jews all over the world. Several months later Idi Amin, the butcher of Uganda, was overthrown. He found refuge in Saudi Arabia.

In 1996, Yoni's brother, Benjamin Netanyahu, defeated Shimon Peres and became Prime Minister of Israel.

The C-130 Hercules transport plane in which the Israel commando forces were flown to Entebbe.

The Israel–Egypt Peace Treaty / 1979

In May 1977, Israeli voters elected a new government. The Likud, headed by Menachem Begin (1913–1992), became the largest party in the Knesset.

Menachem Begin wanted peace for Israel, and he hoped that he and President Anwar Sadat of Egypt might reach an agreement. In November 1977, for the first time ever, an Arab leader, President Sadat, visited Jerusalem. Sadat addressed the Knesset on his wish for peace.

In 1979 Begin and Sadat met at Camp David in the United States. There, with the assistance of President Jimmy Carter, they hammered out their many differences. On March 26, 1979, they signed a peace treaty in Washington, D.C.

The other Arab states bitterly opposed the Camp David Agreement. They swore to take revenge on Sadat for having negotiated with the Jewish state. In October 1981, he was killed by an assassin's bullet and was succeeded by Hosni Mubarak.

Hosni Mubarak

Hosni Mubarak, the new President of Egypt, soon became the target of Islamic extremists, partly because he maintained diplomatic relations with Israel. His corrupt government offered little hope of a better life for the poor Egyptian people.

Despite severe repression and countless death sentences, Muslim fundamentalists have waged an ongoing war of terror against the Mubarak regime, targeting government officials and Coptic Christians. On June 15, 1991, Hosni Mubarak escaped an assassination attempt in Ethiopia.

The Two Faces

The President of Egypt has been the most vocal defendant of the Palestinians. He has organized anti-Israel conferences and accused the Israelis of human rights violations. President Mubarak has urged the Arabs to resist Israel with violence.

Left to right: Begin, Carter, and Sadat after the peace treaty was signed in Washington on March 26, 1979.

Hosni Mubarak

Mission to Iraq / 1981

Ever since the beginning of the conflict with Israel, the Arab countries have been able to obtain the most up-to-date weaponry—short of nuclear arms. In 1980 the Israeli government grew very anxious over reports that Iraq was developing nuclear, chemical, and biological weapons. Israel was especially concerned about the nuclear production facilities in Osirak, 10 miles from Baghdad.

On June 7, 1981 Israeli aircraft flew about 600 miles through enemy air space and bombed the Iraqi nuclear facility. The plant was destroyed and all the aircraft returned safely.

The whole world condemned Israel, but secretly most of Iraq's neighbors applauded the raid, since an Iraq armed with nuclear bombs would have been a threat to the whole region. The full benefit of the raid on Osirak was seen during the 1991 Persian Gulf War. Iraq used biological weapons against U.S. troops, and might have used nuclear weapons if they had been available, but fortunately, thanks to Israel, it had none.

President Saddam Hussein of Iraq launched an ambitious program to modernize his arsenal of offensive weapons. He built chemical, gas, and biological weapons and used them against the Kurds and Iranians. In addition, he began building a nuclear weapons facility at Osirak. In 1981 an Israeli air attack destroyed the half-built reactor.

Peace for Galilee / 1982

Lebanon is a pipeline terminus for oil coming from Saudi Arabia and Iraq. Before 1970, it was a very prosperous and modern country with a highly skilled and educated work force. Its capital, Beirut, was the banking, commercial, and resort center of the Middle East.

Things began to change in 1970 when the Palestine Liberation Organization, now headed by Yasir Arafat, was expelled from Jordan and set up a base in Lebanon. Israeli settlements along the Lebanese border came under frequent rocket and artillery attack. The residents of border towns in Galilee had to live in shelters because of the PLO bombardments.

Israel—Lebanon

In 1975, a brutal civil war broke out between Lebanon's Christians and Muslims. After many battles and thousands of casualties, the Syrians moved in and restored order. They became the power behind a new Lebanese government. The Syrians allowed the PLO to continue its attacks on northern Israel, which became more and more intense.

Finally, on July 6, 1982, The Israeli army launched Operation Peace for Galilee. Under the command of General Ariel Sharon, Israeli troops pushed into Lebanon and captured Beirut. Many of the PLO terrorists and their Syrian allies were killed or captured. A large amount of guns, tanks, and missiles was also taken.

Most of Lebanon's Christians were happy to see the Israelis. They had been robbed and beaten by the PLO and the Syrian troops. Now, thanks to the Israelis, they once again had some security. Prime Minister Menachem Begin hoped that the PLO threat would be ended once and for all. But Operation Peace for Galilee caused much controversy. Many foreign governments objected, and thousands of Israelis protested as well.

Israel Withdraws

In 1983 the Israeli troops were withdrawn and Begin resigned. A small contingent of Israeli troops and Christian Lebanese militia maintained a small security zone on the frontier to prevent terrorist infiltration into Israel. Despite the troops there are still enemy incursions and rocket attacks on the towns of northern Israel.

General Ariel Sharon commanded Operation Peace for Galilee.

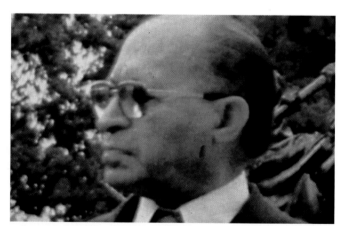

Menachem Begin headed the Betar movement in Poland before he was 20 years old. Because of his Zionist activities, the Russians sentenced him to a Siberian labor camp. In 1942 he immigrated to Palestine, where he organized the armed Jewish underground struggle against the British. He evaded the police by disguising himself as a bearded rabbi. Begin founded the Herut (Freedom) Party and in 1977 became Prime Minister.

Israel and the Gulf War / 1991

In July 1990 President Saddam Hussein of Iraq threatened to use force against any Arab country that continued to pump oil above its OPEC quota. The price of a barrel of oil had fallen from $20 to $13. Each dollar dropped meant a $1 billion loss for Iraq. The Iraqi threat was especially aimed at the adjoining kingdom of Kuwait.

On August 2, 1990, 100,000 Iraqi troops invaded Kuwait and quickly took control of the country. Six hundred oil wells were set afire. Torture, killings, mass arrests, and looting of anything of value continued without a stop. The whole world condemned the invasion except King Hussein of Jordan and the PLO. On August 7, 1990 President George Bush set in motion Operation Desert Storm under the command of General Norman Schwarzkopf. A huge airlift of soldiers, arms, and ammunition began flowing into staging areas in Saudi Arabia. Egypt, Saudi Arabia, and most of the countries of Western Europe joined the coalition against Iraq.

Israel, however, was not part of the coalition because the Arab members did not want to be seen fighting side-by-side with Israel against their Arab brothers. President Bush extracted a promise from Prime Minister Yitzhak Shamir not to take military action against Iraq even if Israel was attacked.

Scud Missiles Hit Israel

On the first night of the war, eight Iraqi Scud missiles hit Israel, two in Haifa, two in Tel Aviv, and four in unpopulated areas. As the missiles fell, Arabs in the West Bank watched from their rooftops and cheered.

Saddam Hussein fired a total of 86 Scud missiles, 40 at Israel and 46 at Saudi Arabia. Some were intercepted by U.S. Patriot missiles. In Israel 250 people were wounded. In and around Tel Aviv about 9,000 apartments were damaged. The most lethal Scud attack was on a U.S. barracks in Saudi Arabia; 28 Americans were killed.

Iraq's defeat in the Gulf War had important consequences for Israel. The PLO lost the financial backing of Saudi Arabia and Kuwait because it had supported Saddam Hussein. Weakened by its loss of funding, the PLO was for the first time willing to begin peace negotiations with Israel.

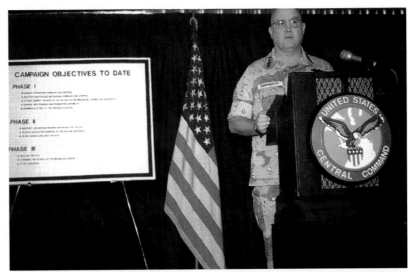

General Norman Schwarzkopf explains the aims and objectives of Operation Desert Storm.

The Peace Agreement / 1993

The Middle East Peace Conference convened in Madrid, Spain, in 1991. While further meetings were taking place in Washington in 1992, a tiny group of PLO and Israeli delegates met secretly in Norway. Their discussions continued for 15 months. On September 13, 1993, Prime Minister Yitzhak Rabin of Israel and Yasir Arafat, head of the PLO, signed a peace agreement in Washington.

Some of the terms were:

1. The PLO would have jurisdiction over the city of Jericho and the Gaza Strip.

2. The PLO would have jurisdiction over police, fire, health, water, and education.

3. Israel would have jurisdiction over borders, roads, and the protection of Jewish settlements in the PLO enclaves.

4. A phased Israeli troop withdrawal would begin on December 13, 1993. Within nine months Israel would withdraw from all West Bank cities. Soon after that it would transfer all remaining land except the Jewish settlements to the Palestinian National Authority.

5. The final status of the territories would be settled at the end of five years.

On September 3, 1993, the Israeli Knesset, which has 120 members, approved the peace agreement by a vote of 61 to 50. Although all Israelis yearn for peace, many did not trust Arafat and the PLO, and felt that Israel was giving up too much too soon. Victory came, as expected, from the 44 members of Rabin's own party, 12 votes from the leftist Meretz party, and 5 votes from the Israeli Arab Knesset members. Without the Arab votes the agreement would not have been ratified.

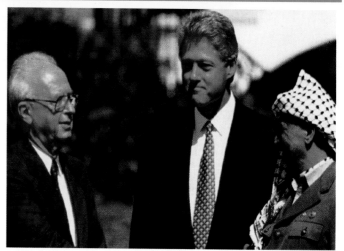

Prime Minister Yitzhak Rabin, and Yasir Arafat in Washington. President Bill Clinton negotiated a handshake between these two enemies.

Qalqilya

As part of the agreement, Israel agreed to withdraw the IDF from six major Arab cities in Judea and Samaria: Qalqilya, Ramallah, Jenin, Bethlehem, Tulkarm, and Hebron. Israel has kept its part of the agreement, and has withdrawn from all cities. As part of its agreement, there is a small detachment of Israeli troops to protect the 450 Jews who live in Hebron.

The Oslo accords stipulated that Israeli troops would withdraw from all West Bank cities. Israeli troops have not been withdrawn from Hebron because of the danger from the hostile Arab population.

Reasons for the Agreement

On September 13, 1993, Prime Minister Yitzhak Rabin and Yasir Arafat signed a peace agreement in which Israel and the PLO recognized each other's right to exist. The negotiations for this historic agreement took place in Norway over a period of 15 months. After so many years of warfare the two combatants decided, each for its own reasons, that it was time to call a halt and seek an accommodation.

The Palestinian Reasons

1. Hamas, the extremist party, was getting stronger and gaining more and more recruits. The influence of the PLO was slowly being eroded. In time its ability to command the loyalty of the Palestinians would disappear. Its prestige would be restored if it gained control of part of the occupied territories.

2. The PLO government in exile was bankrupt. During the Gulf War, the PLO had sided with Iraq against Kuwait and Saudi Arabia. At the end of the war the two kingdoms cut off their financial support for the PLO. As a result, the destitute PLO had not paid its employees and military personnel for many months. Without financial support, it would have to close its offices and disband its guerilla troops.

3. During the Cold War the Russians had supported the PLO politically in the United Nations. They had also supplied it with weapons and money. Now that the Soviet Union had broken up and the Cold War had ended, Russia lost interest in the Middle East and the PLO. As a matter of fact, several of the states of the former Soviet Union were having their own problems with Muslim extremists.

The Israeli Reasons

The Israelis also had some special reasons for seeking a peaceful, though imperfect, solution to the Palestinian problem.

1. Israel had been at war for 45 years since 1948, and many Israelis were psychologically and physically tired. Three generations of Israelis, grandparents, parents, and children, had tasted the bitterness of war, and a majority of them were ready for some sort of compromise.

2. Hamas, the extreme wing of the Arab liberation movement, was gaining strength. Its terrorists were totally dedicated to the destruction of Israel. The security situation within Israel would worsen if Hamas gained control of the Arab masses.

3. Hundreds of thousands of Russian immigrants had come to Israel. Many of them were highly educated and skilled professionals. Israeli economists believed that peace with the neighboring Arab countries would provide a beneficial dividend. Israel would be transformed into a high-technology center for the entire Middle East and thus be able to provide work for the immigrants.

Israeli and Palestinian policemen on joint patrol.

History of Hebron

The ancient city of Hebron is located 19 miles south of Jerusalem, in the Judean Mountains. It is the site of the Cave of Machpelah, revered by Jews as the burial place of the Patriarchs and Matriarchs. Muslims venerate it as Al Haram Al-Ibrahami, the Tomb of Abraham.

Hebron was destroyed by the Romans in the 1st century C.E., and the Byzantines built a Christian church on the site of the Cave of Machpelah. After the Arab invasion in the 8th century, Caliph Omar, the Muslim ruler, allowed Hebron's Jewish inhabitants to build a synagogue near the cave. The Muslim conquerors converted the Christian church at the cave into a mosque.

They built a wall at the entrance of the cave, in which they put a small window through which Jews could pray. A decree prohibiting Jews and Christians from entering the holy shrine remained in effect until 1967, when Israeli troops captured Hebron during the Six-Day War.

The Destruction of the Jewish Community

In 1929, the Jews of Hebron were attacked by an Arab mob. In the riot, during which the British police refused to intervene, 69 Jewish men, women, and children were murdered. The Jewish community of Hebron was totally destroyed.

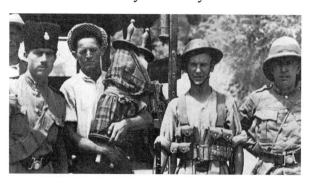

The Arab rioters in 1929 demolished or burned all of Hebron's synagogues. This Jewish survivor managed to salvage a Torah scroll from the ruins of a synagogue.

The Cave of Machpelah

As result of the Six-Day War, Hebron came under Israeli rule. In 1972, Jewish settlers established the community of Kiryat Arba half-mile from the Cave of Machpelah.

Seven years later, in 1979, Rabbanit Miriam Levinger led a group of women and children into Hebron, where they re-occupied the old Hadassah Hospital in the Jewish quarter, which had been destroyed in 1929. By 1994, the Jewish community of Hebron numbered more than 400.

Baruch Goldstein

On February 24, 1944, Dr. Baruch Goldstein, a resident of Kiryat Arba, entered the Cave of Machpelah and killed 29 Arabs. He himself was beaten to death. In contrast, to the massacre in 1929, this incident was the act of one deranged individual. In the aftermath, the Israeli government apologized for the murders, and has paid compensation to the families of the victims. Nevertheless, Goldstein's grave has become shrine to many Jews.

Hebron Today

The Palestinians insist that the Jewish settlers must be removed from Hebron, so that it becomes an entirely Arab city. The Jewish inhabitants say that they have the right to live anywhere that they wish. Benjamin Netanyahu and Yaser Arafat have concluded an agreement whereby the Jews of Hebron can continue to live there.

Israel and Jordan / 1994

When Israel became independent in May 1948, Jordan's Arab Legion joined in the attack on it and occupied East Jerusalem, Judea, and Samaria. Jordan gave citizenship to thousands of Arab refugees from Israel. After the Six-Day War in 1967, Jordan lost control of Jerusalem, Judea, and Samaria to Israel, but its population still included a huge number of Palestinians. In September 1970—known in the PLO's annals as Black September—Yasir Arafat and his guerilla fighters tried to overthrow Hussein's government. Syria planned to invade Jordan at the same time, but was prevented by the threat of Israeli intervention. Thanks to Israel's support, the Arab Legion crushed the Palestinian revolt. The PLO, expelled from Jordan, found a new base of operations in Lebanon.

On October 26, 1994, Prime Minister Yitzhak Rabin and Prime Minister Abdul Salam Majali of Jordan signed a peace agreement. The two countries are cooperating in the development of water resources, transportation, postal service, and telecommunications, and have agreed to alleviate the human problems caused by the Middle East conflict. Israel and Jordan have exchanged ambassadors. King Hussein reacted positively to the election of Prime Minister Benjamin Netanyahu in 1996, in part because of concern that a PLO state on the West Bank would be as much of a danger to Jordan as to Israel.

King Hussein has shown his skill as a survivor on the Arab political map. The King is now mending his fences with the PLO and Yasir Arafat. In September 1996 he made an appearance with Arafat and voiced his support for the political ambitions of the PLO.

King Hussein

March 13, 1997
A Jordanian soldier opened fire and killed seven girls from an orthodox Jewish high school, and wounded eight. In a gesture of consolation, King Hussein visited the bereaved families and offered his heartfelt apologies and condolences.

Signing the peace treaty between Israel and Jordan. President Clinton (*front row, center*) and Secretary of State Warren Christopher (*rear row, second from left*) participated in and signed the agreement.

Syria and Israel

Peace Talks Between Israel and Syria

Since 1991 Syria and Israel have been holding peace talks, in which Damascus has demanded full Israeli withdrawal from the Golan Heights. Israel has called for normalized relations, open borders, and diplomatic recognition. Prime Minister Rabin indicated a willingness to withdraw from the Golan in stages over a period of eight years, but Syria demanded immediate full withdrawal or nothing. On July 12, 1995, the Israeli-Syrian peace talks in Washington were terminated, and the delegates returned home.

The Grapes of Wrath

In April 1996, Hezbollah, a Palestinian guerilla organization backed by Iran and Syria, fired hundreds of Katyusha rockets into northern Israel from its bases in Lebanon, forcing the evacuation of thousands of Israelis. Israel retaliated with a massive air and artillery bombardment called Grapes of Wrath. Unfortunately, thousands of Lebanese civilians were affected by the fighting and fled northward.

Warren Christopher

American Secretary of State Warren Christopher made a series of more than 20 diplomatic trips between Damascus and Jerusalem. After numerous meetings President Assad agreed to a ceasefire. The terms of the agreement localized the hostilities into the Israel-held strip in southern Lebanon. On May 30, 1996 the day of the Israeli election, Hezbollah once again attacked, wounding four Israeli soldiers.

Unsettled conditions, with periodic outbreaks of fighting, continue on Israel's northern border.

Many observers feel that Syria is not really interested in making peace.

Archeologist have identified several ancient synagogues on the Golan Heights. Five have been partially excavated. The best-preserved synagogue in the Golan is near the capital Katzrin. An Aramaic inscription was found in the building: "Uzi made this square." The building was partly destroyed in the 7th century C.E., and in the 13th century it became a mosque.

In recent decades, the Israelis have rediscovered its great wine-making tradition. The Golan Heights cooperative is located near Katzrin, the capital of the Golan. It produces quality wines under 3 labels: Yarden, Gamla, and Golan. All of Golan's wines are kosher, since only Jews are involved in all stages of production.

Jerusalem and the Arabs

One of the most important issues in the Arab-Israeli dispute is the control of Jerusalem.

This holy city has always played a central religious and political role in Jewish life. King David recognized its importance and made it the capital of ancient Israel. King Solomon made Jerusalem the religious center of Judaism by erecting the Holy Temple there. According to rabbinic tradition, Jerusalem is the center of God's spiritual world.

During the 2,000 years of exile, Jews never lost their love for the holy city. As they were led into Babylonian captivity in 586 B.C.E., they tearfully sang:

If I forget thee, Jerusalem,
May my right hand lose its cunning,
May my tongue cleave to its palate.

There are many references to Jerusalem in the daily, Sabbath, and holiday prayers. Worshippers in the synagogue always face toward Jerusalem.

In every generation there has been a Jewish presence in Jerusalem. Jews continued to worship at the ancient Western Wall. Because of the tears of exile, the Wall was often called the Wailing Wall.

As part of the 1949 armistice agreement, the United Nations split Jerusalem into two parts, the New City to be controlled by Israel, the Old City and its holy shrines, by Jordan. The agreement stated that Jews would have free access to worship at the Western Wall and the shrines in the Old City.

In spite of the agreement, the Jordanians did not allow Jews to worship at the Western Wall. To further aggravate the situation, they vandalized the Jewish cemetery on the Mount of Olives and destroyed many of the Old City's historic synagogues.

In 1967, during the Six-Day War, Israel captured the Old City and reunited Jerusalem.

Jerusalem is sacred to three religions: Judaism, Christianity, and Islam. The Israeli government guarantees all religions freedom of access to their holy places and shrines. Everyone is free to worship God in complete freedom.

The Muslim View of Jerusalem

The two holiest cities of Islam are Mecca and Medina. Mecca is where Muhammad, the founder of Islam, was born. Medina is where he preached and developed the Muslim religion. Jerusalem is also considered a holy city by Muslims, although its role in the earliest years of Islam was comparatively minor.

Muslims believe that Muhammad, in a dream, was transported up to heaven from the Temple Mount in Jerusalem. In the 7th century, several decades after the Muslim conquest of Jerusalem, Caliph Abd Malik ibn Marwan built the Mosque of Omar on the site where Muhammad's dream was said to have occurred—the exact spot

The Old City of Jerusalem is divided into four sections or quarters: Jewish, Arab, Christian, and Armenian. The Christian quarter contains many churches, schools, and important historical and religious sites.

where the First and Second Temples had stood some 1,600 years earlier.

Jerusalem and the Palestinian Authority

The Palestinians insist that East Jerusalem must be the capital of the state they hope to establish on the West Bank. Israel maintains that Jerusalem is and will always be Israel's capital—to quote Yitzhak Rabin, "Jerusalem is the ancient and eternal capital of the Jewish people."

Because of these seemingly irreconcilable positions, the peace treaty with the PLO refers to Jerusalem in deliberately vague language. Israeli and Arab diplomats hope to solve the questions pertaining to the holy city before the treaty goes into full effect.

Jerusalem and the United States

Despite the bonds of friendship between Israel and the United States, the U.S. government continues to locate its embassy in Tel Aviv. The State Department refuses to recognize Jerusalem as the capital of Israel. In addition, it maintains a separate American consulate in East Jerusalem for the convenience of Palestinians.

The U.S. Senate has passed a resolution which requires the the State Department to move the American embassy to Jerusalem, but no steps in this direction have been taken.

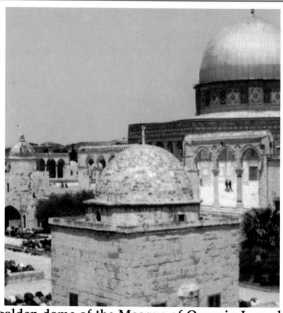

The golden dome of the Mosque of Omar in Jerusalem is a highly visible landmark. It was built by Caliph Abd Malik ibn Marwan in 691 C.E.

POPULATION MAP OF THE LARGEST CITIES IN ISRAEL

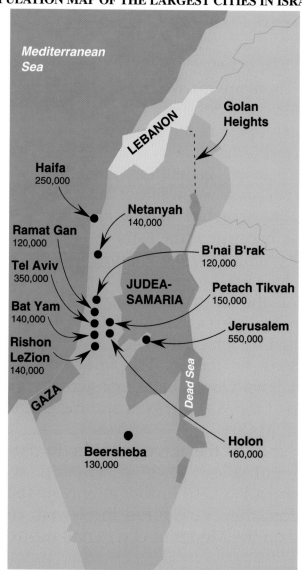

Mediterranean Sea

LEBANON

Golan Heights

Haifa
250,000

Netanyah
140,000

Ramat Gan
120,000

B'nai B'rak
120,000

Tel Aviv
350,000

JUDEA-SAMARIA

Petach Tikvah
150,000

Bat Yam
140,000

Jerusalem
550,000

Rishon LeZion
140,000

GAZA

Dead Sea

Holon
160,000

Beersheba
130,000

The Knesset building in Jerusalem. The Knesset is the legislative body of the State of Israel. Its 120 members are elected by a secret ballot.

The Assassination of Yitzhak Rabin / 1995

Saturday night, November 4, 1995, was one of the most fateful times in the history of modern Israel. On that darkest of nights, Yitzhak Rabin, Israeli's Prime Minister and one of its great military heroes, was assassinated.

That evening 100,000 Israelis had assembled in Tel Aviv to participate in a political rally. Rabin delivered a speech and joined in singing the "Song of Peace." After the rally Rabin and Shimon Peres began to walk to their cars.

Lurking in the dark shadows of the night, a young assassin named Yigal Amir was waiting. As Rabin approached his limousine, Amir quietly stepped out of the shadows and from about a yard away pumped three bullets point blank into the Prime Minister.

Rabin was rushed to a nearby hospital, where he died on the operating table. The shocked nation went into mourning, and the spot where Rabin was shot became a shrine filled with memorial candles, flowers, and posters.

Rabin's funeral was attended by President Bill Clinton, former Presidents Bush, Carter, and Ford, and the leaders of many other countries, including President Mubarak of Egypt and King Hussein of Jordan. Rabin was succeeded as Prime Minister by Shimon Peres, who vowed to continue his policies.

YITZHAK RABIN (1922–1995) served his country both as a soldier and as a diplomat. Born in Jerusalem, he graduated from the Kadoori agricultural school. In 1940, he enlisted in the Palmach and participated in numerous underground actions against the British Mandate. In 1946, he was arrested by the British and imprisoned for six months. During the War of Independence, Rabin commanded the Harel Brigade, which was active in the battle for Jerusalem. Appointed Chief of Staff in 1964, he led Israel's forces to victory in the Six-Day War of 1967. After serving as Israel's ambassador to the United States, Rabin became Prime Minister in 1974–77 and was reelected in 1992. On November 4, 1995, he was assassinated by Yigal Amir.

Among the foreign dignitaries paying their last respects to Yitzhak Rabin were (*from left to right*) President Bill Clinton, former Presidents Jimmy Carter, and George Bush, Queen Beatrice of the Netherlands, Mrs. Peres and Prime Minister Shimon Peres, Queen Nur and King Hussein of Jordan.

The Election of 1996

On June 2, 1996 Benjamin Netanyahu (b. 1949), of the Likud Party, defeated Shimon Peres and became Israel's new Prime Minister. His victory was in large part due to public disquiet about the way the peace agreement with the PLO was proceeding. While Israel had been carrying out all of its commitments, the PLO was not. It had not modified its covenant to eliminate language calling for the destruction of the Jewish state. Even worse, terrorist attacks had become increasingly more frequent and brutal. While Israelis desperately wanted peace, a majority of voters agreed with Netanyahu that it was necessary to proceed cautiously and slowly, and with more concern for security than Peres had shown.

SHIMON PERES

Shimon Peres had a varied and distinguished political career. At the age of 24 he became the manpower chief of the Haganah. After the formation of the State of Israel he was appointed Director General of the Defense Ministry. In 1981 he became Deputy Defense Minister under Prime Minister David Ben-Gurion and then under Levi Eshkol, and was responsible for setting up Israel's nuclear capabilities. In 1977 he ran against Menachem Begin and lost. In 1988 he ran against Yitzhak Shamir, and also lost.

As Foreign Minister in Yitzhak Rabin's cabinet, Peres conducted peace talks with the PLO which ushered in the Oslo accords for Palestinian self-rule. Prime Minister Rabin and Peres shared the Nobel Prize for their peace efforts.

In 1995, after the assassination of Rabin, Peres became Prime Minister.

The following year he ran against Benjamin Netanyahu but was defeated.

Benjamin Netanyahu

Netanyahu was the first sabra Prime Minister of Israel. Although born in Israel, he lived for several years in the United States and earned degrees in business and architecture from the Massachusetts Institute of Technology. In 1967 he returned to Israel to serve in the army. As an officer in an elite commando unit, he played an important part in the team that rescued hostages from a hijacked Belgian plane in 1972. He served as Israel's United Nations ambassador in the 1980s and was also Deputy Foreign Minister.

Benjamin Netanyahu addresses the U.S. Congress. In the background is Vice President Al Gore. Newt Gingrich, House Majority Leader, congratulates him.

Israeli Politics / 1971–1996

1971

Menachem Begin of the Likud came to power, however, because Likud controlled only 43 of the 120 Knesset votes, it was forced to share power with the Labor Party.

November 1977

President Anwar Sadat of Egypt came to Israel and in September 1978 signed a peace treaty called the Camp David Accords in which the Sinai was returned to Egypt. For their efforts, Begin and Sadat were awarded a Nobel Peace Prize.

1983

Menachem Begin, resigned as Prime Minister and was succeeded by Yitzhak Shamir. Once again a unity government of Likud and Labor was formed. For the first two years Shimon Peres was Prime Minister.

1988

A general election and a new coalition government was formed by Likud and Labor. Yitzhak Shamir remained as the Prime Minister.

May 1989

Prime Minister Shamir called for Arab elections in Gaza and the West Bank. The elected representatives would negotiate a solution to the Arab-Israeli conflict.

January 1992

The first secret meeting between the PLO and Israel took place in Norway. Yossi Beilin, a member of the Knesset and an aide to Shimon Peres, Israel's Foreign Ministe,r was the Israeli delegate.

August 1993

The secret Norway meetings initiated talks on Palestenian self-rule.

September 13, 1993

Prime Minister Rabin of Israel and Chairman Yasir Arafat of the PLO signed a peace agreement in Washington.

October 13, 1993

The Israelis and the PLO met in Tabis, Egypt, and arranged the transfer of authority. Israeli withdrawal from Gaza and Jericho was to be completed by April 1994.

November 6, 1993

The transfer of authority was postponed because of the differences between the PLO's and Israel's interpretations of the peace plan.

December 12, 1993

Prime Minister Rabin and Yasir Arafat decided to postpone the implementation of the Peace Treaty. The murder of numerous Jewish settlers by Arab terrorists had turned the Israeli electorate against the treaty.

December 14, 1993

United Nations adopted a resolution that endorsed the peace treaty between Israel and the PLO.

February 24, 1994

Dr. Baruch Goldstein, a resident of Kiryat Arba, a Jewish settlement on the outskirts of Hebron, entered the Cave of Machpelah and killed 29 Arabs, and was then himself killed. Hebron has had a long history of violence between Jews and Arabs. In 1929

Arabs murdered 69 Jewish civilians. Seven years later, in 1936, the entire Jewish community was destroyed.

May 4, 1994
Premier Yitzhak Rabin of Israel, and PLO Chairman Yasir Arafat signed a self-rule peace accord in Cairo.

November 4, 1995
Yitzhak Rabin was assassinated by Yigal Amir. Shimon Peres assumed the post of Prime Minister.

June 2, 1996
Benjamin Netanyahu narrowly wins a hard-fought victory over Shimon Peres. The upset victory of Netanyahu proved that the Israeli public was aware that the Labor Party had disregarded many of its promises. The vote indicated that a majority of Israeli Jews wanted Israel to remain a Jewish country, a Jewish state with Jewish values, and wished to maintain its Jewish identity.

July 8, 1996
Prime Minister Benjamin Netanyahu visited the United States and had a high-level meeting with President Bill Clinton. The subject was terrorism in the Middle East and the future of the peace accord in Israel.

The Americans were very concerned about the terrorist threat to the political stability of Saudi Arabia, the largest supplier of oil to the free world.

Benjamin Netanyahu indicated that his primary goal was the security of Israel. In addition, he stated in absolute terms that Jerusalem would remain the capital of Israel and would not be divided. He also stated that he was against the creation of a PLO state. In his words, "There is no Palestine."

September 26, 1996
The opening of an ancient tunnel in Jerusalem ignited three days of rioting by the Palestinians.

June 13, 1997
After months of deliberation, the Israeli Parliament, in an 87 to 14 vote agreed to carry out the Israeli–Palestinian Peace Agreement of the previous Rabin government.

Israel has notified the Palestinian Authority that it is prepared to carry out the first of three withdraws as stipulated in the Oslo Agreement. The first withdrawal from nine percent of the West Bank has angered the Palestinians who have demanded a thirty percent slice of the West Bank.

February 4, 1997
At 7:30 in the evening, two Israeli helicopters ferrying 73 soldiers, collided in mid-air over the Northern Galilee, killing every one on board. The helicopters were en route to the Israeli security zone, in Southern Galilee. This accident was the worst military disaster in IDF history.

February 27, 1997
The Israeli Cabinet approved the development of a new Jewish neighborhood in East Jerusalem. When completed, the new neighborhood will contain 6500 apartments and is being built on Jewish owned land in Bar Homa.

The Struggle of Modern Israel

JEWISH HIGHLIGHTS

Displaced Persons	Zionist Spokesman	State of Israel 1948	Six Day War	Yom Kippur War 1976

JEWISH EVENTS • PERSONALITIES • LITERATURE

▷ Haganah	▷ Rabbi Meir Berlin	▷ End of Mandate	▷ Jerusalem liberated	▷ Israeli Olympic athletes mudered
▷ Irgun Zvai Leumi	▷ Abba Hillel Silver	▷ Arabs attack Israel	▷ Yitzhak Rabin Chief of Staff	▷ Kissinger's shuttle diplomacy
▷ Internment camps		▷ Haganah repels attack	▷ Jerusalem Day	▷ Golda Meir resigns
▷ S. S. *Exodus*		▷ Chaim Weizmann President of Israel		▷ Yitzhak Rabin New Prime Minister
		▷ Ben-Gurion Prime Miniser		▷ Golda Meir dies 1978
		▷ Jewish refugees Suez Campaign		▷ Rescue at Entebbe Jonathan Netanyahu dies

WORLD HISTORY

	▷ United States	▷ England	▷ Israel	▷ American Nuclear Alert
		▷ France		
		▷ Suez Canal		
		▷ Egypt		

The Struggle of Modern Israel

JEWISH HIGHLIGHTS

| Israel–Egypt Peace Treaty 1979 | Peace for Galilee | Peace Agreement 1993 | Yitzhak Rabin | Benjamin Netanyahu |

JEWISH EVENTS • PERSONALITIES • LITERATURE

Israel–Egypt Peace Treaty 1979	Peace for Galilee	Peace Agreement 1993	Yitzhak Rabin	Benjamin Netanyahu
Menachem Begin Premier of Israel	General Ariel Sharon	Rabin and Arafat sign peace agreement	Yitzhak Rabin assassinated	Netanyahu meets President Clinton
Sadat comes to Jerusalem Sadat murdered 1981	Begin resigns	Knesset approves peace agreement	Yigal Amir	Anatole Sharansky
Mission to Iraq	Scud missiles attack Israel / 1990	Israelis evacuate six Arab towns	Shimon Peres becomes Premier	Russian Jews continue to arrive
	Patriot missiles protect Israel	Israelis remain in Hebron	Election 1996	Islamic guerrillas attack Israel and America
		Israel and Jordan sign peace treaty	Benjamin Netanyahu defeats Peres	
		Syria and Israel agree not to agree		

WORLD HISTORY

Israel–Egypt Peace Treaty 1979	Peace for Galilee	Peace Agreement 1993	Yitzhak Rabin	Benjamin Netanyahu
Iraq	Gulf War	Syria		United States
Egypt				Russia

Judaism in America

In the early years of the 20th century, many American Jewish young people, the children of immigrants, began to give up elements of their Jewish identity and lifestyle in order to become "like other Americans." This attitude accounts, in part, for the growth of modern denominations of Judaism more attuned to the New World environment.

Assimilation was, and is, widespread, because of the virtually total acceptance accorded minorities in the United States. By the second half of the century, however, many began to realize that America was made up of many diverse groups, all of them of immigrant origin, and that each group, by preserving the best of its own heritage, might add variety and richness to American life—differences, in other words, were respected and respectable.

Rebirth of Identity

As a result, there was a rebirth of Jewish identity and commitment among a substantial minority of American Jews. This was reflected in the 1960s and afterward in the havurah movement on many college campuses, in the baal teshuvah movement that has brought many young people back to Orthodoxy, and in the energetic response to Christian missionary activities.

Though Jews in present-day America are few in number, amounting to less than 3 percent of the population, Judaism is regarded as one of the nation's three great faiths—a key component of its Judeo-Christian heritage. Jewish and Hebraic studies are an important part of the curriculum of many major colleges and universities. In addition, the American Jewish community supports a network of yeshivot and other religious schools.

The Jews of America enjoy freedom, good fortune, and the respect of their neighbors. Organized into Orthodox (1,200), Conservative (800), Reform (853), and Reconstructionist (87) congregations, American Jews regularly unite for purposes of education, social action, and help to the needy. By learning and practicing the Jewish tradition, and by living according to Jewish ideals of justice, they are writing a glorious chapter in the history of their people.

Jews in American Society

After World War II, when the terrible details of the Holocaust were made known, anti-Semitism became a fringe or underground activity. There was a dramatic improvement in publicly expressed attitudes about Jews and Judaism. Quotas restricting the number of Jews in universities, professional schools, and certain jobs largely ceased, although the existence of affirmative action programs on behalf of other minorities has raised concerns in this area. Overall, young people growing up in America today find it hard to believe that their parents and grandparents met prejudice and had to fight discrimination.

The American Jewish Congress, the American Jewish Committee, the Anti-Defamation League of B'nai B'rith, and the Jewish Labor Committee all worked to fight anti-Semitism and to protect the rights of fellow Jews. They lent their support, as well, to the cause of civil rights for all minorities.

Jews play a prominent role in American art, literature, and general culture. They have long contributed to science and medicine, and are active in education, industry, and government.

American Jewry Unites to Give

Throughout the 20th century, American Jewry donated great sums for the relief and rescue of suffering coreligionists. No other group has ever given so much or organized itself in the same manner for voluntary taxation to help needy brethren.

In 1925 the Keren Hayesod, or Foundation Fund, and the Jewish National Fund joined forces and became the United Palestine Appeal. When war broke out in 1939, and the need for rescuing the Jews of Europe became desperate, the Joint Distribution Committee combined its efforts with the UPA. Thus was formed the United Jewish Appeal. The UJA has remained active ever since, helping Jews in every country of the world.

Jewish Philanthropy

In almost every American city, the UJA, the Joint Defense Appeal, and local causes (such as hospitals, Jewish centers, homes for the aged, educational institutions) combined their efforts so that there was one major fund drive for the entire community each year. Generally the umbrella agency conducting the drive is known as a Jewish Federation.

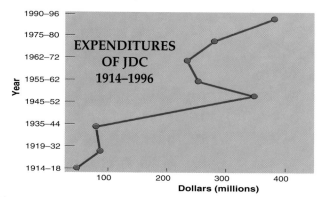

The Joint Distribution Committee has been the most remarkable and far-reaching of all private philanthropies, feeding, rescuing, training, and resettling persecuted Jews all over the world. The amount given by Jews of the democratic countries for JDC activities has increased as the need has grown greater.

Photo taken at the 92nd Street Y in New York, largest and most famous community center in the world and a member agency of New York's Federation of Jewish Philanthropies. The Federation aids Jewish education, hospitals, and other Jewish activities.

In giving to welfare and charity funds, the Jews of America have set an example for all other groups. In the first 20 years after World War II, Jews donated $1.5 billion to the UJA. This generosity is not exclusive to Jewish causes, for Jews have been among the largest supporters of welfare, educational, and cultural projects of all kinds.

American Jews and Israel

Since the State of Israel became a reality in 1948, American Jews have felt a close kinship with the Jews of that land. They show their interest through membership in organizations like Hadassah, through contributions to the United Jewish Appeal, which helps new residents and educates them for citizenship, and by purchasing Israel Bonds and other investments for industrial development.

Defenders of Freedom

Wherever Jews have settled and planted roots, they have participated in the defense of their adopted countries. Even in countries which openly discriminated against them, Jews joined the armed forces and heroically fought for their ungrateful adopted homeland.

There were Jewish soldiers and sailors in the armies of the tsars, the Polish kings, the rulers of Austria–Hungary and pre-Holocaust Germany.

Patriots and Soldiers

In the building of America Asser Levy and his fellow Jews fought for the right to stand guard and protect New Amsterdam against Indian attacks. Although there were only 2,000 Jews in the colonies, they were prominent among the patriots who fought and sacrificed their lives during the Revolutionary War. Francis Salvador, of South Carolina, was one of the first casualties. Haym Salomon is said to have suspended Yom Kippur services to appeal for funds for George Washington's impoverished army in Valley Forge.

Commodores John Ordoneaux and Uriah P. Levy distinguished themselves in battles against the superior British navy in the War of 1812. Abraham Wolfe was killed at the Alamo, during the Texas war of independence. Surgeon General David de Leon acquired the nickname of "the fighting doctor" for his heroic exploits during the Mexican-American War.

The Civil War

Sadly, the Civil War found Jews killing each other on the battlefield. Among the Confederates, there were Judah P. Benjamin, the Secretary of State, and a heroic soldier named Max Frouenthal. His legendary bravery became a symbol of courage for the Confederate armies.

Close to 10,000 Jews served in the Union army, and seven were awarded the Congressional Medal of Honor. 5,000 Jews saw service during the Spanish-American War, and many won medals for courage under fire.

World Wars I and II

During World War I more than 250,000 Jewish men were in the armed services. The majority were in the infantry; 12,000 were wounded or gassed, and 3,500 were killed in action. More than 9,000 Jews were commissioned officers, and seven won Congressional Medals of Honor.

Leopold Karpeles, awarded the Congressional Medal of Honor for bravery in the Battle of the Wilderness, as color-sergeant of the 57th Massachusetts Infantry.

CONGRESSIONAL MEDAL OF HONOR WINNERS

The following American Jews won the Congressional Medal of Honor for valorous deeds and extraordinary bravery in the defense of the United States.

Benjamin Levy	Civil War
Abraham Cohen	*
David Obranski	*
Leopold Karpeles	*
Isaac Gans	*
Abraham Grunwalt	*
Charles Gardner	Indian Wars
David Goodman	*
Jacob Trautman	*
Louis C. Mosher	*
Samuel Gross	Mexican War
William Zion	Peking, China
William Sawelson	World War I
Sydney Gumpertz	*
Benjamin Kaufman	*
Philip C. Katz	*
Samuel Sampler	*
Eduardo V. M. Izac	*
Matt Urban	World War II
Raymond Zussman	*
Samuel G. Fuqua	*
Isadore S. Jachman	*
Jack H. Jacobs	Vietnam

Sydney G. Gumpertz, captain in the 23rd Infantry Division, fought in the Argonne. On September 28, 1918, he single-handedly silenced several enemy machine-gun nests. For his gallantry under fire, he was awarded the Congressional Medal of Honor.

650,000 Jewish men and women served in World War II, and 50,000 received medals and citations for bravery. Lt. Raymond Zussman, a lieutenant in the tank corps, received a Medal of Honor. Zussman's single-handed heroics resulted in the capture of more than 100 Germans and the liberation of a whole town. Sadly, Zussman lost his young life on a battlefield in France. His father had fought in the Russo-Japanese War, and his brother, Abraham, was killed in World War I.

The National Museum of American Jewish Military History in Washington documents and educates the public concerning the courage, heroism and sacrifices made by Jewish Americans who served in the armed forces.

America Honors Its Outstanding Jewish Personalities

The poetess Emma Lazarus wrote, "Give me your tired, your poor, your huddled masses." And millions of Jews, yearning for freedom and opportunity, heeded her words and streamed into the United States. America was good to them, and fulfilled its promise. Through hard work and a desire for education, the immigrants succeeded and built a place for themselves and their children in the land of opportunity.

In turn, the immigrants rewarded America with their patriotism, their genius, and their creativity. The United States post office has recognized and honored some of these outstanding individuals by dedicating postage stamps for their contributions to America.

Walter Lippmann (1889–1974)
Journalist and author

Touro Synagogue
First permanent synagogue in the New World. Located in Rhode Island, it is named after its first rabbi, Isaac Touro.

Bret Harte (1836–1902)
Author.

Benny Goodman (1909–1986)
Musician and band leader.

Charles Steinmetz (1865–1923)
Electrical engineer and inventor.

Joseph Pulitzer (1847–1911)
Newspaper owner and publisher.

Four Chaplains
During World War II Rabbi Alexander Goode and three Christian military chaplains gave their life-vests to wounded soldiers when their transport, the *Devonshire*, was torpedoed.

Al Jolson (1886–1950)
Star of stage, screen, and radio.

Adoph Ochs (1858–1935)
Publisher and owner of the *New York Times*.

Bernard Revel (1885–1950)
Orthodox rabbi and president of Yeshiva University

Fanny Brice (1891–1951)
Singer and comedienne.

George Gershwin (1898–1937)
Composer of operas and musical comedies and film scores.

Albert Einstein (1878–1955)
Physicist. Developed theory of relativity.

Haym Salomon (1740–1785)
Revolutionary War patriot.

Samuel Gompers (1850–1924)
Labor leader and first president of the American Federation of Labor.

Jewish Nobel Prize Winners

Alfred Nobel, a Swedish industrialist, established the Nobel Prize. The prestigious annual awards are given to individuals from all over the world who have made special contributions to humankind.

The following is a list of the Jewish winners. Jews have been awarded more than 100 Nobel prizes. Jews are less than 1% of the world's population, yet they have made up more than 15% of all recipients.

NOBEL PRIZES, awarded annually to men and women who have "rendered the greatest service to mankind." Since the inception of the prize in 1899, it has been awarded lo the following Jews or people of Jewish descent:

World Peace
1911 Alfred Fried
1911 Tobias M. C. Asser
1968 René Cassin
1978 Manachem Begin
1986 Elie Wiesel
1994 Shimon Peres
1994 Yitzhak Rabin
1995 Joseph Rotblat

Literature
1910 Paul J. L. Heyse
1927 Henri Bergson
1958 Boris Pasternak
1966 Shmuel Yosef Agnon
1966 Nelly Sachs
1976 Saul Bellow
1978 Isaac Bashevis Singer
1981 Elias Canetti
1987 Joseph Brodsky
1991 Nadine Gordimer

Physiology or Medicine
1908 Elie Metchnikoff
1908 Paul Ehrlich
1914 Robert Bárány
1922 Otto Meyerhof
1930 Karl Landsteiner
1931 Otto Warburg
1936 Otto Loewi
1944 Joseph Erlanger
1944 Herbert S. Gasser
1945 Ernst B. Chain
1946 Hermann J. Muller
1950 Tadeus Reichstein
1952 Selman A. Waksman
1953 Hans Krebs
1953 Fritz A. Lipmann
1958 Joshua Lederberg
1959 Arthur Kornberg
1964 Konrad Bloch
1965 François Jacob
1965 Andre Lwoff
1967 George Wald
1968 Marshall W. Nirenberg
1969 Salvador Luria
1970 Julius Axelrod
1970 Sir Bernard Katz
1972 Gerald M. Edelman
1975 David Baltimore
1975 Howard Temim
1976 Baruch S. Blumberg
1977 Rosalyn S. Yalow
1978 David Nathans
1980 Baruj Benacerrof
1984 Cesar Milstein
1985 Joseph Goldstein
1986 Rita Levi-Montalcini
1986 Stanley Cohen
1989 Harold Varmus
1992 Edwin Krebs

Chemistry
1905 Adolph Von Baeyer
1906 Henri Moissan
1910 Otto Wallach
1915 Richard Willstaetter
1918 Fritz Haber
1943 George de Hevesy
1961 Melvin Calvin
1962 Max F. Perutz
1972 William H. Stein
1977 Andrew Schally
1978 Daniel Mathias
1979 Herbert Brown
1980 Paul Berg
1980 Walter Gilbert
1982 Aaron Klug
1989 Sidney Altman

Physics
1907 Albert A. Michelson
1908 Gabriel Lippmann
1921 Albert Einstein
1922 Niels Bohr
1925 James Franck
1925 Gustav Hertz
1943 Otto Stern
1944 Isidor Isaac Rabi
1952 Felix Bloch
1954 Max Born
1958 Igor Tamm
1959 Emilio Segrè
1960 Donald A. Glaser
1961 Robert Hofstadter
1962 Lev D. Landau
1965 Richard P. Feynman
1965 Julian Schwinger
1969 Murray Gell-Mann
1971 Dennis Gabor
1973 Brian D. Josephson
1975 Benjamin R. Mottleson
1976 Burton Richter
1978 Peter Kaitea
1978 Arno A. Pensias
1979 Sheldon Glashow
1990 Jerome Friedman
1995 Martin Perl
1995 Frederick Reines

Economics
1970 Paul A. Samuelson
1971 Simon Kuznets
1972 Kenneth J. Arrow
1975 Leonid Kantorovich
1980 Lawrence R. Klein
1987 Robert Solow
1990 Harry A. Markowitz
1990 Merton H. Mille
1992 Gary Becker

Lubavitch in the Twentieth Century

After the death of the Besht in 1760, Dov Ber, the Maggid (preacher) of Mezerich (1710–1772), became the second leader of Hasidism. One of his disciples, Shneur Zalman of Lyady (1745–1813), established his own movement. His book, the *Tanya*, became the foundation of Lubavitch Hasidism. Based on his teachings, this movement is also known as Habad Hasidism, an acronym made up of the first letters of three Hebrew concepts central to its doctrines, *hokhmah* (wisdom), *binah* (understanding), and *da'at* (knowledge).

Rabbi Menachem Mendel Schneerson, 1902–1994

(Messiah) and eagerly expected him to declare himself. When he died in 1994 without doing so and without a direct heir, the movement experienced a difficult adjustment. Nonetheless, it continues to be active and effective in hundreds of Jewish communities throughout the world.

Under the dynamic leadership of Rabbi Joseph Isaac Schneerson (1880–1950), a brilliant administrator with an outstanding talent for communal and civic activities, Habad Hasidism resisted the Soviet government's efforts to stamp out religion. Arriving in the United States in 1940, he steadily built up the Habad movement in this country, establishing yeshivot, a publishing empire, schools for Jewish youth, and an outreach program.

In 1950 Rabbi Menachem Mendel Schneerson (1902–1994) became the seventh Lubavitch Rebbe. He continued the work of Rabbi Joseph Isaac, creating a huge outreach program with mitzvah tanks and Lubavitch centers in hundreds of cities in the United States and all over the world, especially in Russia and Poland. In addition to its synagogues, university Habad houses, yeshivot, schools, and outreach programs, Lubavitch was also involved in rehabilitation and drug outreach programs.

Many Lubavitch adherents believed Rabbi Schneerson to be the Moshiach

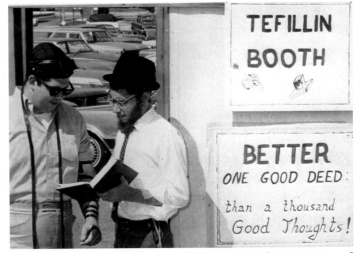

Lubavitch mitzvah tanks travel throughout the country and invite Jews to put on tefillin, light Sabbath candles, reciting blessings over the lulav and etrog, and light Hanukah candles.

Lubavitch representatives use a variety of vehicles to service outlying Jewish communities. The representatives from Minneapolis use a chartered plane for a trip to LaCrosse, Wisconsin.

WORLD JEWRY: *The Jews of Mexico*

Overall, the world Jewish population at the end of the 20th century amounted to about 14 million. The largest Jewish communities were in Israel (5 million), the United States and Canada (6 million), and Russia (800,000). There were another 1.7 million Jews in Europe—half a million in France, many of them immigrants from North Africa, and about 350,000 in Great Britain. The Jewish community of South Africa, though much smaller, was well organized and had many ties with Israel. In Latin America, where about 500,000 Jews resided, the largest community was in Argentina. Lacking adequate religious leadership, the Jews of South America looked to the United States and Israel to provide them with rabbis and teachers.

There have been Jews in Mexico since 1521, when Hernando Cortez and his tiny army, which included a number of Marranos, destroyed the mighty Aztec empire and founded the colony of Nueva España (New Spain). The Inquisition soon extended its reach to the New World, but despite persecution Jews managed to survive and to engage in trade and commerce. Some even held government posts.

In 1821, Mexico gained its independence from Spain. Years of chaos and dictatorship followed. During the presidency of Benito Juarez a civil war broke out, and in 1862 Archduke Maxmillian of Hapsburg, supported by Napoleon III of France, became emperor of Mexico. Maximillian's personal physician was Samuel Bosch, a Jew from Austria, and during his reign Jewish immigration to Mexico increased.

Hernando Cortez (1485–1547) conquered the Aztec civilization of Mexico by 1521. In addition to this, set up colonies as far north as California.

The country's Jewish populace continued to grow and prosper after Juarez overthrew Maxmillian in 1867. The brutal pogroms in post–World War I Eastern Europe induced many more Jews to see Mexico as a safe haven. Numbers of them settled in Mexico City, where they prospered despite the growing anti-Semitism and the imposition of a quota on Jewish immigration. The pace of immigration picked up after World War II.

Most of the country's Jews are concentrated in Mexico City, where the many educational and religious institutions reflect their ethnic and religious diversity. There are Ashkenazi, Sephardi, German, Hungarian, and Syrian synagogues as well a great variety of cultural institutions. Mexican Jews sponsor many cultural and artistic activities.

WORLD JEWRY: *The Jews of France*

Jews first made their appearance in France sometime in the 4th century. Although in the rest of Europe their presence was restricted, in France the Jews were active as merchants and as doctors.

In 1096, members of the First Crusade attacked and killed Jews, and local bishops and rulers were powerless to protect them. The 11th and 12th centuries are called the Golden Age of France. Scholars such as Rashi, Rabbenu Gershom, and the tosafists established schools and produced a treasure house of important literature. Unfortunately, anti-Semitism in the form of forced conversions, blood-libels, and well-poisonings, plagued the Jewish communities and often led to murder, expulsion and book-burnings.

In 1306 King Philip IV banished more than 100,000 Jews and seized their business assets and properties.

Ten years later they were readmitted and once again active Jewish communities sprang to life in many French cities. However, in 1394 Charles VI once again expelled the Jews, and for 200 years they were almost non-existent in France.

Following the expulsion from Spain in 1492, Marranos began to arrive and because of their skills and business connections were welcomed with open arms. In 1648, the Chmielnicki massacres in Ukraine sent a wave of Jews into Alsace–Lorraine. By 1800 there were about 40,000 Jews living there, and by decree they were freely allowed to practice their Judaism.

French Anti-Semitism

Even though French Jews had complete civil rights they often found their upward mobility curtailed by prejudice. In 1894 Captain Alfred Dreyfus, a Jew, was convicted on a charge of espionage. Finally in 1906, he was declared innocent and reinstated. The Dreyfus Affair brought anti-Jewish discrimination in France to the surface and provoked bitter debates.

During World War II the Vichy regime cooperated with the Nazis and deported 80,000 Jews to death camps. French President François Mitterand declared July 16, the anniversary of the arrest of Jews in 1942, as a yearly "national day" for the commemoration of the anti-Semitic persecutions by the Vichy government.

Relations with Israel

The Jews of France have strong personal ties with Israel. The peace negotiations between Israel and the PLO were unpopular, especially among North African Jews and Israeli representatives were publicly attacked.

France as of 1996

France is home to the fourth-largest Jewish community in the world. It is the home of 600,000 Jews, 200 synagogues, 100 day schools, 200 afternoon schools, and more than 500 Jewish organizations. These groups are a rainbow of communal, social, professional, and religious organizations.

Over the years the French Jewish community has included many prominent personalities. Among them are Nobel Prize winners Henri Bergson, and René Cassin. André Citroën founded the automobile company that bears his name. Three Jews, Léon Blum, René Meyer, and Pierre Mendes-France served as Premier. Numerous other Jews have achieved prominence in government service, in the arts, and in commerce and industry. Jewish tradition in France is strong. However, intermarriage is making inroads into the Jewish community.

WORLD JEWRY: The Jews of Canada

The earliest records of Jews in Canada date back to the 18th century, when England and France fought for mastery of the northern part of the New World. Among the officers on the staff of Britain's General Amherst during the French and Indian War were three Jews: Aaron Hart (1724–1800), Emmanuel D. Cordova, and Isaac Miramer.

In 1750, after Canada became an English possession, a number of Jews settled in Montreal. Some of them were fur traders, others were veterans of the British army that had defeated the French. Montreal's first synagogue, Shearith Israel, was established in 1776. Most of the members were of Sephardic ancestry and followed the Sephardic rite.

In 1807 Ezekiel Hart (1767–1843), a son of Aaron Hart, was elected to the legislature of Lower Canada (now the province of Ontario). He refused to be sworn in on a Christian Bible, and instead took the oath on a Hebrew Bible with his head covered. This raised a storm of protest and he was expelled from the legislative chambers.

Years of agitation followed, and in 1832 a bill was passed extending the same political rights to Jews as to Christians. Since that time Jews have won seats in all of the provincial legislatures and in the Federal Parliament, have served as mayors of Toronto, Vancouver, and other cities, and have been judges in courts at all levels. In 1970 Boris Laskin became the first Jewish member of Canada's Supreme Court.

Jews were also very active in Canada's commercial life. Jewish merchants set up general stores in small railroad towns and were also active in the fishing industry, telegraph communications, and the fur trade. Jews participated in the gold rush in British Columbia in 1858. This led to the erection of a synagogue in Victoria in 1862.

Many Jewish refugees came to Canada during and after World War II. Substantial numbers of French-speaking Jews from North Africa settled in French-speaking Quebec in the 1950s and 1960s.

Canada has the fifth-largest Jewish population in the world. The Canadian Jewish community, 350,000 strong, has developed a dynamic educational system comprising 100 schools attended by 20,000 students. There are yeshivot, teachers' seminaries, and a great variety of cultural, religious, and Zionist organizations. The majority of the country's Jews reside in Montreal, Toronto, and Winnipeg, and are active in all phases of communal life.

Jews have made great contributions to Canada's economic, political, communal, and artistic life. Among the more well known Canadian Jews are the novelist Mordecai Richler (b. 1931), Rabbi Reuven Bulka, and philanthropist-communal leader Charles and Samuel Bronfman.

Samuel Bronfman,
Canadian industrialist and philanthropist.

WORLD JEWRY: The Jews of Russia

Since the beginning, the lives of Russian Jews have been difficult and permeated with anti-Semitism. Each of the governing regimes, from the tsars to the Communists, have imposed restrictions on economic opportunities and on Jewish cultural and religious expression.

Leon Trotsky (Lev Davidovich, 1879–1940) was exiled to Siberia in 1898 for revolutionary activities, but in 1902 he escaped to England. During the October Revolution in 1917 he returned and played an important part in the Communist uprising. Leon Trotsky organized the Red Army. In 1929 he was exiled by Stalin and went to Mexico, where he was murdered by the Russian secret police. To the very end he was antagonistic to Judaism. Leon Trotsky, seated in the center, is shown with a group of army officers, some of whom were Jews.

During the black years of the Stalin era, from 1919 to 1953, Soviet Jewry was decimated, first by the Nazis and then by the Communist regime. Over half of Russia's enormous Jewish community, which at one time totaled over 5 million, was murdered in the

Joseph Stalin (1879–1953) ruthlessly eliminated all of his political rivals after the death of Lenin. The police state he created murdered more than 20 million Russians.

Holocaust. At the end of World War II, Stalin launched a campaign to destroy Jewish cultural and religious identity. Tens of thousands of Jewish intellectuals and professionals were murdered, and hundreds of thousands were exiled to Siberia in a wave of terror.

Stalin's death brought some relief, but official anti-Semitism still limited Jewish economic, cultural, and religious life. The establishment of the State of Israel in 1948, awakened a spirit of hope and the struggle for the right to immigrate. Jewish refuseniks led by Anatole Sharansky challenged the regime by organizing hunger strikes and secret groups for the teaching of Judaism.

Golda Meir, Israel's first ambassador to the USSR, mobbed by Moscow Jews outside the synagogue, Rosh Hashanah, 1948.

By the end of the 1970s, the USSR was in an economic crisis and the political infrastructure was in a state of collapse. When Mikhail Gorbachev became Premier, in 1985, he set in motion the policy of perestroika (reorganization) and removed all emigration barriers. Gorbachev's policy of glasnost (openness) officially permitted cultural, religious, and political activities and unloosened a flood of Jewish emigration to Israel, America, and other countries.

328

Boris Yeltsin

The reelection in 1995 of President Boris Yeltsin was much better than a loss could have been. Yeltsin's opponents conducted a campaign filled with smears and open anti-Semitism and a loss could have had a catastrophic affect on Russian Jewry. As of 1997, Jews, despite the bureaucracy, were free to emigrate to Israel and anywhere else they pleased.

Internally, the Russian Jewish community is making progress. Individual groups are pooling their resources under an umbrella organization called the Russian Jewish Congress. Their aim is threefold: fund-raising, fighting anti-Semitism and Jewish education.

Russian and Israeli authorities have established transit schools called Ma'ariv schools to facilitate those intending to make aliyah. These schools, much like an American day school, provide a secular program as well as a Hebrew language and Judaic studies curriculum.

Jewish culture and religion are being introduced and spread by Orthodox, Lubavitch, Conservative, Reconstructionist, and Reform groups. They have organized a rainbow of synagogues and managed to attract thousands of worshippers.

Jewish sports clubs—a part of the Maccabee movement—attract 50,000 youngsters with a variety of programs. In addition to sports, the youngsters are exposed to Jewish music, culture, and religious activities.

For more than 70 years Russia was a Jewish cultural desert. Now, through the committed efforts of world Jewry, the Russian Jewish community, which some believe numbers about 1.5 million, is slowly making progress and struggling to regain its former stature.

Boris Yeltsin

The United Jewish Appeal has established a youth program called Naaleh, ("we will go up"). It sends thousands of Jewish teenagers from Russia to Israel, to complete high school and prepare for college. This experience has encouraged many of them to settle in Israel.

The Joint Distribution Committee has throughout the years shipped matzot to Russia for Passover. With the help of the JDC, local committees in the former Soviet Union are producing their own. This matzah factory in Kiev provides for the needs of Jews in Ukraine, Belarus, and Moldova.

WORLD JEWRY: *The Jews of Israel*

On May 14, 1948, the fifth day of the Hebrew month of Iyar, in the year 5708, according to the Jewish calendar, Israel gained its independence. On this great day, David Ben-Gurion announced, as if an answer to the familiar Hebrew prayer, that the new state would be open for *Kibbutz Galuyot*, the Ingathering of the Exiles.

In the years that followed, hundreds of thousands of Jews of different cultures, different languages, different worlds, streamed into the Jewish homeland. Never before in the history of the world had so many people from so many different lands descended so quickly upon so small an area.

Today Israel's population is close to 5 million Jews, and the diversity of its people makes the country almost like a miniature United Nations.

In addition to its Jewish citizens, Israel also has more than a million non-Jewish citizens, mainly Muslims, but also including Christian Arabs and Druze. Under Israel's democratic system, all citizens have full political and civil rights.

Ashkenazim

About half of Israel's Jews are the children and grandchildren of German and Eastern European Jews. They are called Ashkenazim, from the Hebrew word *Ashkenaz*, the name for the area that is now northern France and Germany. Most of the Zionist settlers who built up Palestine were from Eastern Europe. Many other Ashkenazim found freedom and security in Israel after the bitter sickness of the Nazi Holocaust in Eastern Europe.

Many Ashkenazim especially the Hasidim, speak Yiddish, a language which combines Hebrew and German words. Yiddish developed during the years of Jewish exile in European countries.

The Sephardim

Sephardim and Oriental Jews make up the other half of Israel's Jewish population. Sephardim are descendants of the Jews expelled from Spain in 1492 by King Ferdinand and Queen Isabella. These Jews scattered to many countries, but since they were originally from Spain they were called Sephardim, which in Hebrew means "Spaniards." Many Sephardim speak Ladino, a language which combines Hebrew and Spanish words, just as Yiddish combines Hebrew and German. Ladino developed during the years when Jews lived in Spanish-speaking countries.

Newly arrived Russian Jewish immigrants to Israel. More than 500,000 Russians have found new homes in Israel. As the political situation in Russia deteriorates, many new arriving families are welcomed.

Oriental Jews

Many of Israel's Jews are immigrants from Oriental countries like Iraq, Yemen, Kurdistan, Persia, Afghanistan, Morocco, Libya, Tunisia, and Algeria. The special expertise of the craftsmen from these countries is renowned , and the souvenir shops of Israel are filled with jewelry and metal sculptures that capture the spirit of the Orient in their delicacy and precision.

Sometimes Oriental Jews are called Sephardic Jews, although in actuality their backgrounds differ, since unlike the Sephardim they are not descended from ancestors who once lived in Spain and Portugal.

The Sabras

The Ashkenazic, Sephardic, and Oriental Jews of Israel are not separated by geographical barriers the way their ancestors once were. They live side by side in Israel. Their children play together in the same kindergarten classes and attend the same high schools; they grow up together in the same neighborhoods and youth groups, and serve together in Israel's army regiments. They all speak modern Hebrew in the same Sephardic pronunciation.

As the distinctions between the groups blur, Jews born in Israel no longer identify strongly as Ashkenazic, Sephardic, or Oriental; instead, they are sabras, native-born Israelis with their own Israeli culture—an amalgam of all three immigrant groups, plus a touch of something uniquely Israeli.

The term *sabra* is a nickname for Jews born in Israel. The sabra is a desert fruit that grows on cactus; it is hard and prickly on the outside but soft and juicy on the inside.

Ethiopian immigrants on an Israeli air force plane from Addis Ababa to Israel during Operation Solomon.

The thorny sabra plant and its sweet and juicy fruits. Native Israelis are called sabras because they are thorny on the outside, but friendly when you get to know them.

WORLD JEWRY: *The Jews of Latin America*

The history of Latin American Jewry began in 1492, when Christopher Columbus arrived in the West Indies with several Marrano seamen in his crews. In the next few decades, due to the excesses of the Inquisition, many New Christians from Portugal and Spain made new homes for themselves in Brazil, Mexico, and Peru.

The arrival of the Inquisition in the New World meant that the Marranos once again had to lead double lives. Despite the difficulty and danger, many of them remained faithful to their Jewish identity and secretly kept up Jewish traditions and customs, including holiday observances and the dietary laws. Thousands of New Christians were punished and many burned at the stake for their adherence to the Jewish faith.

During Latin America's wars of independence from Spain between 1808 and 1826, freedom of religion was introduced. In 1816 Argentina, Mexico, Peru, and Uruguay abolished the last symbol of Spanish oppression—the Inquisition.

Due to the more favorable conditions, Jewish immigration to Latin America increased, spurred especially by the severe oppression in Russia and Eastern Europe. Most of the newcomers settled in Brazil and Argentina.

Baron Maurice de Hirsch
Immigration to Argentina was encouraged by Baron Maurice de Hirsch, who in 1891 purchased more than 500,000 acres of land there and donated $10 million, a huge sum in those days, to set up the Jewish Colonization Association (ICA). The ICA funded a number of agricultural colonies in Argentina, and by 1925 there were 30,000 Jews engaged in farming and cattle ranching. Colonization attempts were also made in Bolivia, Mexico, Ecuador, and Uruguay, but these initiatives failed.

The Jewish farmers in Argentina encountered many difficulties, and today most of the country's Jews are concentrated in the big cities, especially the capital, Buenos Aires.

Between 1901 and 1914, as conditions in Eastern Europe deteriorated, immigration to Argentina reached a high of more than 100,000 new arrivals. The rise of Nazism in the 1930s, when the need for a safe haven was greatest, tragically witnessed a decrease in Jewish immigration, for the Argentine government instituted a series of restrictive immigration laws. Despite this, some Jews managed, both legally and illegally, to settle in Argentina, and others found their way to Brazil, Panama, Chile, Bolivia, and Ecuador. Today there are 500,000 Jews living in Latin America. Most of the Jewish communities in Latin America enjoy middle-class status and stable economic conditions. They are active in manufacturing, communications and in the professions.

Anti-Semitism has always been a serious problem in Argentina, sometimes from Nazi sympathizers, other times from radical leftists. On March 17, 1992 a massive terrorist bomb destroyed the Israeli embassy in Buenos Aires.

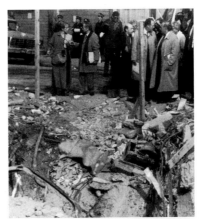

Jewish delegations from all over the world flew to Buenos Aires to offer their support to the survivors. The seven-story headquarter of the Jewish Mutual Aid was reduced to rubble. One hundred people were killed and more than 200 were wounded.

Index